COULD IT BE LOVE 2
A NOVEL
SLAYED BY STACEY STAXX

Star City Publications
P.O Box 7322
Harrisburg, Pa 17113
www.starcitypublications.com
www.StaceyStaxx.com

ISBN- 13: 978-0-9833860-8-7
ISBN- 10: 0-9833860-8-0
First printing 2016
Printed in the United States of America

20 1 1 9 0 2 7 4 0

Acknowledgements

Thank you to all of my family and all of my real supporters, this all has been a great blessing to me. I wouldn't have been able to do this without God, because man God is good! And secondly without my 85k and plus supporters, my squad my team who goes super hard for me and who I will go hard for as well. This is just the beginning of my journey and everyday with improvement and the joy, it will only get better….

To all of my readers, which is too many to name you all are special to me and mean so much to

me please sign your name here___________________________________

To my family, the ones that support me. (Looking) Thank you lol. :-) So loves here is my second book and I hope you all enjoy this, just know I had a hella good time writing this, it took me through all types of emotions, so jump on this roller coaster and enjoy!

STACEY MOTHER FUCKING STAXX! TWO X'S :-)

BOOK COVER MODELS, THANK YOU FOR GRACING MY COVERS, YOU BOTH ROCKED AND I CAN'T WAIT TO WORK WITH THE TWO OF YOU AGAIN!

Cherie
Email : bookingcherie@gmail.com
Instagram : cherie.vie

ishakeythemodel
Booking info: ishakeybennett@icloud.com

Love is still conquering it all. In this second part of this dangerous love affair, secrets are revealed, hearts are broken, families are torn apart and friendships are broken as well. With secrets being revealed, Luke questioned if what he had with Taylor could it be love or is it just pure lust. JaKai now has two women that is dangerously in love with him, who will he give his heart to? Or will he be able to give his heart to anyone. Michelle, beyond delusional, confused and angry at the world, she won't stop until she gets what her hearts want, after all the heart knows what the heart needs and want. Will she finally give up on love or will love give up on her? Love is a dangerous game and sometimes love could get you killed. Take a ride with this gang of lovers on this deeply wild and emotional rollercoaster.

This book is dedicated to anyone who has fallen deeply in love and felt like they lost all hope, getting tangled in someone else, losing all control of yourself. Love yourself, always and forever…

Could It Be Love 2

INTRO
PART 1

Nia decided to get up and get ready for school. She knew she was late but she didn't give a damn. She would rather be fashionably late than never. She took her time to do her makeup and to get dressed and an hour later she was walking through the cafeteria doors. She couldn't wait to see Taylor and tell her all about her little bundle of joy. She was in a better mood than before and decided that she wasn't going to abort her baby after all. She was going to raise her child by any means and be a damn good mother, with or without JaKai.

As soon as she stepped foot inside the cafeteria all eyes were on her. Continuing, Nia heard all the whispering, laughing and saw all the finger pointing. "What the fuck is funny?" Nia blurted. She sat alone, next to a wall plug to place her cellphone on the charger. Seconds later her phone powered on. Seeing a request from a page Facebook page with her picture on it she became curious as hell. She accepted the request and wanted to see who was trying to steal her identity. She looked at the page and noticed that it had over 500,000 followers. "Okay a bitch steals my photos and is popping with over five kay followers! Shit, the bitch better give me a shout out or something," Nia said to herself. She scrolled down the page and her eyes lit up. Her mouth flung wide open when she saw the video of her and JaKai fucking. It had over 2 million views, 250,000 likes and over 10 thousand comments. Tears ran down Nia's face. She looked up and noticed all eyes and nasty stares were gearing towards her.

"NIA, IN MY OFFICE, NOW!" She heard the principal yell.

She stood up snatching her phone plug out the wall and took off running. She was so hurt and so embarrassed that she wanted to die. She couldn't believe that the world saw her fucking and sucking all over Facebook. Her life would never be the same. She was probably already labeled the biggest hoe there was.

She was distraught and she wasn't thinking straight. Rushing into the house, she ran upstairs. She swung her closet door open and pulled out a wire clothes hanger. Then she'd gone into the bathroom and stripped. Standing in the tub she didn't give it any thought. She viewed videos of home abortions many of times to where she felt like she had it all down packed. It looked easy and simple. She stuck the clothes hanger inside of her canal and when feeling like it was hooked on something, she yanked it so hard that she thought she had snatched her uterus out. "AHHHHHHH!" Nia yelled in agony. She dropped the hanger and blood squirted from between her thighs. She looked down and felt like she was about to pass out. That wasn't enough for her. She wanted to die. Death was knocking right at her door. Blood dripped all over her floor.

She ran downstairs and pulled a chair from out of her kitchen and had gone through the living room closet until she found a laundry line to tie a knot in it.

"OH GOD, WHAT HAVE I DONE?" She cried. Tears and snot graced her face. She was shaking badly. The state of mind that she was in at the moment was dangerous to society and even worse to herself. Nia stood on the chair and removed a few of the ceiling tiles. Underneath them displayed a 4x4 wooden stick. She threw the rope over it and tied the knot around her neck. She said a quick prayer. She was afraid but didn't think again about what she was about to do. The devil was riding her and had her exactly where he wanted her. Nia kicked the chair away from her and her body hang limply and lifeless from the ceiling…

INTRO
PART 2

One thing had led to another and before Taylor knew it, JaKai had her lying across the bed with her legs up in the air as he dug deep inside of her sweet pussy with his hot tongue. He was like crack and she was like the addict who was trying to get herself clean but everything the crack came into her possession she couldn't turn that glorifying last hit. She felt so bad but she just couldn't turn the shit down. "Oh damnnnn JaKai I feel so bad." Taylor cried.

JaKia ignored her and kept on eating the hell out of her pussy like it was the best thing he ever tasted.

*****

Michelle woke up the next day feeling joyful. Feeling as though she'd been in the best mood ever she dressed and made her way home. She didn't think about the damage she'd done to Nia and her reputation. Nor did she give a damn. She was out to destroy the girl by any means, all due to her man not knowing how to keep his dick in his pants. Michelle felt like why the hell should anyone else in the world be happy if she was one of the most miserable beings to grace earth? Uh huh, no way in hell was anyone in her presence going to happy until she got her happiness and life in tact. She was one selfish being and it had always been that way. It was always about MICHELLE! MICHELLE AND MICHELLE!

*****

JaKai had Taylor bent over and was digging her out from the back. He was pounding her insides so hard that he thought he was going to kill her. He made a promise to himself that as much as he wanted Taylor, after this time he was going to have to let her go. He loved his right hand and he loved Nia. When he put his heart on the line, the winner was Nia by a long shot. He just had to get the last of Taylor out of him and after that he was good. He was just about to cum when he heard a door slam closed. Looking out the window he noticed Michelle's car. He had to think quickly. There was no way Michelle was going to go for Taylor being with Luke and being left there. He figured if he told the truth shit was going to get ugly no matter what. He looked over at the closet then back Taylor.

"Is someone coming?" Taylor asked.

JaKai nodded. "Get in the fucking closet!" He blurted.

I can't believe this nigga got me hiding in the fucking closet! I should have never answered that damn bathroom door, she thought as she rolled her eyes. She ran her hands through all of the hanged designers and kicked a pair of off black Prada shoes when she saw them. Had she seen Michelle's closet weeks ago she would have been even more mad. She was just pure jealous that JaKai was giving this bitch any and everything that she wanted when she on the other hand was the one that was going beyond measures by fucking him. Not to mention the videos that she allowed him to record of her like she was a porn star. She just couldn't put her hands on it but when it came to JaKai it was hard for her to tell him no. Minutes ago he had her doing all sorts of things that she couldn't imagine herself doing in a million years. The powerful hold of her that he had drove her insane at times, yet she couldn't break the army chains that were wrapped around her entire body. She made millions of promises to herself that she was going to never betray the ones who she loved and who loved her dearly, and to do right by them. But not today. JaKai caused her to break those promises. She huffed, blowing her hair away from her oval shaped face. Her grey eyes sat alert as she stood there in her nudeness. She thought back to just how seconds ago that she was getting piped down as JaKai slid his long thick member in and out of her, fucking her insanely, to now being shacked up in his closet while he argued with Michelle.

"I FUCKING HATE YOU JAKAI!"

Taylor listened as JaKai and his wannabe wife went back and forth. She eased out the closet a bit and scanned the bed where all her belongings were underneath. Just as she was about to step out the closet she heard footsteps coming her way.

"DID YOU CATCH ME CHEATING MICHELLE? NO YOU DIDN'T SO CHILL THE FUCK OUT BABY." JaKai told his wife.

Taylor rolled her eyes. She badly wanted to step out the closet but she didn't just yet.

JaKai walked closer to Michelle and grabbed her by the sides of her face. He licked his tongue across his lips and went in for a kiss. Their tongues locked and he lifted her long dress above her head, exposing a perfect pair of D cups and a nice freshly shaven kitten. Leaning down he took her breast in his mouth one by one.

"You make me sickkkk." Michelle moaned. Minutes later Taylor was watching as JaKai fuck the life out of Michelle just the way he had done her.

The way he stared her in her eyes as he rammed his thick member in and out of her canal, to the slushing noises of wetness and love filled the air all made Taylor sick. She looked on with tears in her eyes as Michelle climbed on top of JaKai.

"Oh gawd baby I loveeee youuuu!" She cried as her double D jugs bounced up and down in the air.

Taylor couldn't take it any longer. Her heart was beyond broken. All of their dirty secrets were about to come out of the closet as she opened the door...

The vibrating of her cellphone caused her to step back and she glanced down at it on the floor. Quickly she picked it up before the sound could be heard coming from within the closet. "SHIT." She cursed underneath her breath. '*Taylor, you are the best thing that happen to me since the night I met. These streets don't have no type of love for a nigga. Let's make what we have official. Lets make this Taylor and Luke against the world type of shit. You got a nigga in his feelings.*' Taylor read the message from Luke. Tears ran down her cheeks as she began to feel so low down for what she'd been doing lately, when she had a good man who wanted her. But the dick JaKai was slanging was so damn good that she was fucking sprung. She was so caught in her feelings that she didn't see the closet door being swung open.

"JaKai how dare you bring this bitch in OUR home?" Michelle screamed. She quickly snatched a hanger from the closet. "Bitch you are going to pay for this!" She raised that hanger and went to town on Taylor's naked ass.

Taylor was helpless. Her phone dropped and she fell back, taking a handful or more clothing with her.

Jakai came running from out the bathroom when he heard all the commotion.

"I HATE YOU JAKAI! I SWEAR ON MY BABY Y'ALL ARE DEAD!" Michelle cried. She climbed across the bed and headed towards her nightstand she opened the drawer and pulled out her small 380 and aimed it towards the closet.

Taylor's eyes lit up when she saw the gun. She couldn't believe that she had gotten caught in the middle of JaKai's shit. She knew that Michelle must've thought she was Nia and now her hot pussy was going to cost her deadly. She threw her arms up in the air. "It's not what you think." She said.

Michelle wasn't trying to hear what she was saying. She closed her eyes and squeezed the trigger! BOOM! The gun went off!

"NOOOO!" JaKai screamed. Things were spiraling out of control right in front of his eyes. He didn't know what had gotten into him and what had gotten into Michelle. He kind of figured that LOVE itself was driving Michelle insane. A long time ago, he was warned by his mother about females like Michelle. He didn't see it but many others always told him that Michelle was crazy and they could see it embedded in her eyes. Today he saw firsthand for himself that she was beyond crazy and even more she was crazy in love, which would make one do any-damn-thing without giving it any thought.

He jumped in front of Taylor and the bullet ripped right through his flesh. "AHHH!" He screamed.

Taylor was scared like hell. She looked at JaKai with tears in her eyes. He mouthed the word 'run' to her. Taylor's heart was racing a million miles per second. She felt like her heart was going to give out at any second. She didn't know whether or not JaKai was dead.

"OH MY GOD, JAKAI!" Michelle screamed and dropped the gun. "BITCH LOOK WHAT YOU MADE ME DO!"

Taylor quickly snatched her clothes and shoes up. With her phone in her hand she didn't give it any second thought. She took off in the nude and ran. No track star had shit on her ass, she ran until she got out of sight. Running across the street naked, she didn't see the car coming full speed towards her. She was caught in the headlights like a damn deer.

CHAPTER 1

Luke whipped and weaved through traffic like a bat out of hell. The only thing that was on his mind was Alesha and her well-being. His baby sister, he loved her with all his heart. Hell his heart beats for her. He made a promise to her, his mother and himself that he was always going to be there for Alesha no matter what. He seen so many fatherless girls in his life and the damage that was done to them and vowed to protect Alesha from all of that. So he played a father role in her life, her big brother and a best friend when she needed one.

He pulled up to the hospital and jumped out the car, leaving it parked at the Emergency entrance.

Running like hell he burst through the hospital doors.

"Luke!" He heard his mother yell his name.

He rushed to her side. "Where is she?" He asked.

His mother began crying. "They just got her stabilized. They had to rush her off to emergency surgery."

Luke looked at her and squinted his eyes. "Momma what's going on?"

She shook her head. "I don't know, Luke. I know they found her at Morning Star. I think..." She sighed. "I think she was in the process of getting an abortion and it went bad."

Luke covered his mouth with his right hand and took a seat to place his face in the palms of his hands. Shaking his head, he thought about how Alesha said she needed the money for cheerleading, and after he gave her the money he knew damn well she was lying. She was hiding something and asked for just enough for an abortion. Hell when she asked him for that particular amount it should have hit him hard, being that he saw JaKai dish it out to numerous females who slipped up and got pregnant.

"FUCK ALESHA!" Luke yelled while banging his hand on the seat.

Two hours later, Alesha was out of surgery and was taken to another part of the hospital where she received her blood transfusion. The doctors had to surgically removed the rest of the fetus from her uterus, but with all the blood that she lost, she had to get an emergency blood transfusion. Luke and his mother walked into her room side by side.

Alesha was awake but very drowsy and weak. Her heart melted when she saw the two who loved her more than life itself. "I'm so sorry Luke," she spoke, noticing the distraught look on his face. She knew he was very upset with her and more than likely hurt by her actions and decisions. "It only happened one time and one time led up to a big accident. I know you must hate me." She began to cry.

Luke rushed to her side. "Nah I don't hate you at all," he told her. "I hate that little mother fucker who got my baby sister knocked up. I hate the fact that you couldn't come to me and talk to me about your situation." He then reached in for a hug and embraced her.

Alesha looked up at her mother. "Momma, I just knew you wouldn't understand. I didn't know how to tell you and most importantly I didn't want to break your heart, because I knew I failed you."

"Failing me is when you give up," she cried. "And you have never given up Alesha. I love you and I love Luke. This was all a mistake and we as humans tend to make mistakes. You live and you learn. My main concern is your health and I'm glad you are okay now. I don't know what I would do if anything happened to any of my babies."

The three hugged each other tightly and shared a few tears.

Luke's cellphone rang and he ignored it by looking at the screen and turning it off. "Well since we are all here gathered in this small ass room, I got some big and good news to tell ya'll." He said.

Both his mother's and Alesha's eyes lit up. "What, you won the Powerball last night? Are we millionaires?" Alesha blurted in excitement.

Luke playfully nudged her. "Nah, big head!" he said. "A nigga wish, though. But nah, you two are going to be an auntie and a grandmother." He smiled.

"Oh my God Luke! Are you fucking serious!" Alesha asked. "Oops." She looked at her mother when she realized she slipped up and said a curse word. Their mother didn't play that shit at all. She didn't dare allow her children to sit around her and use profanity. That was complete disrespect. "Are you serious Luke." Alesha corrected herself.

Luke nodded. "Yup. I just found out today."

His mother was smiling ear from ear. "About damn time. When do we meet her? Why haven't we met her yet? How old is she? What's her name? What is she like? What is her family like?" She asked a mouthful.

Alesha smile., "I met her momma, she's really pretty, smart and she ain't one of them hood chicks that you been warning Luke about."

Their momma playfully pouted. "And why haven't I met this special lady yet?"

Luke looked at her. "You will meet her next weekend. I'm planning a special dinner for her at the house." He didn't want to answer any of his momma's questions. She would just have to meet Taylor for herself.

While Luke and his mother discussed Taylor, Alesha took the time to grab her phone and text the man who she was deeply in love with. With age playing a big factor between the two of them, love wasn't permitted. Alesha had met Johnathan— better known as Streets— on the street a few months ago. She and her girlfriends were skipping school and were hanging out on the block which was something that Alesha didn't normally do. Since Streets and his boys spotted group of girls they had their eyes on them. It was obvious that the girls were young but with the bodies of some baddies, and Streets and his boys didn't give a fuck.

Instead they approached them.

"Ya'll trying to smoke with us or what?" One of Alesha's hot in the ass friends asked.

"Hell yeah!" One of Streets boys spoke. He looked the young girl up and down and already knew what it was hitting for.

All six piled up in Streets' van and ended up stopping to get some Loud and some liquor. They drove back to one of the trap houses that they hustled out of.

While everyone indulged in getting high and drunk, Alesha sat off to the side to herself and played games on her cellphone.

Streets stood back, watching her. He was instantly taken aback by her beauty and the way she carried herself. She was obviously different from the rest. He had just come home from prison and wasn't into settling down but Alesha was someone he could see himself creating a future with.

Streets made his way over to Alesha. Hovering over of her he scoped out her voluptuous set of breast that were cuffed tightly in her tank top. He licked his lips. He was turned the hell on. Thoughts of him taking Alesha in the back room and lying her on the old dirty mattress that was held up by four bricks crossed his mind. But nah, he wanted something better for Alesha. She was too damn fine for that quick, rough and raunchy shit. When he got ahold of her he wanted to turn her into a lady. His lady at that.

"What you playing? Miss Anti-social." Streets flirted, sitting down next to Alesha.

She shrugged. "Candy Crush." She replied.

He smiled, staring into her brown bedroom eyes. "Why you ain't over there with your friends?"

Alesha glanced over at the girls who seemed to be having a good time. "I don't drink or smoke."

Impressed, Streets nodded. "Then let's get out of here and catch a matinee."

Alesha gave it a quick thought. Her heart started to flutter because a boy was asking her out on a date… or wasn't it a date? No matter what it was, she grabbed her things and she and Streets left out the house.

He was sweet and kind to Alesha; she had him doing things that he normally didn't do. Like hold the door open for her, whisper sweet things in her ear, paying for her movie ticket, popcorn and stuff. Like hell if he would do those things normally for a female. In his eyes, he saw females as nothing but gold digging bitches and tricks. But being around Alesha made him want to refrain from thinking as such. After the movies Streets took Alesha back to his mother's house. Things were sprouting so quickly for the two of them.

They lay across the bed with her legs thrown behind her head. "Ohhhh." Alesha cooed as she experienced being oral sex for the very first time.

Streets took his time and licked her from her clitoris to her asshole. With the fresh scent of her pussy he could tell that it was never touched. The way his tongue tightly squeezed inside of her canal he knew she was a virgin.

Alesha gyrated her hips and grabbed the sheets. "Johnathan! Ohhhh, Johnathan!" She cried in lust. Her thighs tightened around his neck, and her first orgasm rained all over his tongue.

Streets crawled between her legs and planted kisses on her stomach. Making his way up, he softly sucked on her breast. He wanted to bless every inch of her body. Their lips met and Alesha experienced her first kiss. Streets had her on Cloud 9.

"I'm a virgin," Alesha softly spoke.

Streets smiled. "I'm going to take it easy."

He spread her thighs a bit. "Ouchhhh!" Alesha cried.

Streets took his time sliding his dick inside of her, and a few seconds later he was deeper than he'd been. He made love to her. He stared deep into her eyes, and if only their eyes spoke…the things his eyes was saying to her. That quickly, some good pussy and an innocent young girl had Streets in love.

Alesha's walls tightly wrapped around his member. He couldn't contain himself not even five minutes into her sweetness; he was busting a load all up inside of her. He fell down beside her and held her tightly into his arms. "You're my lady, and this here is mine." He told her placing a kiss on her cheeks.

Needless to say exactly a month later, Alesha's period was a no show. She grabbed three pregnancy tests and they all read positive.

Her emotions were all over the place. Had her brother and her mother found out, she would have been dead for sure. She thought about her education and her life ahead of her; she couldn't be a mother. She was way too young.

She had cut Streets off completely, and blocked his number. Not giving up, Streets was heartbroken. Alesha had him head over heels. After attempting to contact her on numerous occasions he wasn't giving up… until Alesha changed her number on him.

Now being pregnant, Alesha had no choice but to con Luke out of the money and get rid of her problem before anyone found out…

Alesha sighed and thought about what she was going to say to Streets. Speaking from her heart she began texting him. '*Hey this is Alesha. I know it's been a while since you heard from me but I wanted to let you know that I was pregnant with your child. I got scared, not knowing what to do or how you would have taken it. I attempted to get an abortion which almost cost me my life. Now I'm laid up in the hospital, lost and confused. I don't know what I did— if I made the right decision or not. I fell in love with you and I wanted to protected our love. Had my family found out, it would have been really ugly. Maybe you will forgive me, maybe you won't. Regardless, I wanted to let you know what happened Johnathan, and no matter what... I love you.'* She pressed send on the phone then placed it back on the stand beside her bed.

"Are you hungry?" Luke asked Alesha.

She smiled and nodded. "Yes, can we get some Chinese?"

Luke nodded and ordered food for the three of them. They sat, talked, laugh and caught up on old times.

CHAPTER 2

"Don't hit me!" Taylor screamed with her hands up in the air.

The driver swerved a bit and slammed on breaks. "Are you fucking crazy?" The lady screamed jumping out the car.

Taylor rushed up to her side with a face full of tears. "I'm so sorry." She cried.

The lady scanned her. It was obvious that Taylor had just been through hell. "Are you okay? Can I do anything to help you? Are you going to put your clothes on?"

Taylor nodded and quickly put her clothes on. "I'm fine now, I just need a ride." She told the lady.

The lady thought about it being a setup. Perhaps Taylor was trying to rob her or something. Looking at her again, she could tell that the youth was harmless. Innocent and naked and afraid was written all over her face. "Come on." She told Taylor.

Taylor got into the car. "Thank you." She said.

She then used the woman's phone to call 9-1-1 for JaKai. She didn't know whether he was dead or alive. The sad thing was that she cared for him and it didn't help that she gave the operator the wrong number.

"You are my savior," she told the lady while directing her to Nia's house. She thought about going home, but then didn't want to deal with her parents who were overly possessive. She called Luke back to back but he hadn't answered. So she had no choice but to head to Nia's. On her way to the house, Taylor stared out the window. She had such an ill feeling but didn't know what it was. When she pulled up the lady looked over at her. "Thank you so much." Taylor said.

"You are welcome and I hope everything works out for the best for you. Just make sure you be careful honey." The lady smiled, glad she was able to be a good Samaritan and help someone out who was truly in the need of help.

"I will be." Taylor said easing out of the car. Just as she was getting up, Nikki pulled up in an all black Navigator. "Hey Nikki." Taylor waved.

Nikki smiled. "Hey Taylor. What, you skipping school again? You ain't tired of your parents beating that ass yet?"

"I'm going to be grown soon and I will be on my own."

Nikki nodded. "Don't grow up too fast." She told her.

"I"m trying not too but my parents are forcing me too."

"I understand but one day you'll be thanking your parents for being hard on you. I know sometimes it drives you crazy. Just follow their rules until you are able to be on your own."

Taylor shrugged.

"Have you talked to Nia's ass today? I swear she better not have one of them grown ass boys up in here."

Earlier that day she had gotten a call from Nia's school stating that she had come in late and left shortly after she arrived. They also said they had some disturbing things involving Nia and they needed Nikki to come back the next day with Nia to have a sit down with the principle.

"Earlier and that was it. Only through text." Taylor told her.

The two of them walked up the steps. Nikki stuck her key in the doorknob. "She better have a damn good excuse as to why I have to carry my ass up to that school tomorrow."

She was never the type to be too hard on Nia. In fact she allowed Nia to do as she pleased as long as she respected her and didn't cause her to go out of her way to do things. She was pissed that she had to take off to attend Nia's school for a sit down. She knew Nia was fast in the ass but never did she have to meet up with any of her teachers, so it bothered her that Nia could have possibly done something out of the ordinary. She turned the doorknob and her and Taylor walked in the house.

The sight before them sent Taylor to vomiting all over herself, and Nikki could barely move. Taylor's high pitch scream brought her back to reality. "AHHH OHHHH GOD! NIAAAAAA!" Taylor screamed at top of her lungs.

Nikki and Taylor both rushed over to Nia who was hanging lifeless from the ceiling. Blood trickled down her legs. The horrid sight that was before their eyes was a sight that no mother or best friend should ever have to see.

"Oh my God! Do something!" Nikki screamed to Taylor, rushing over to her daughter.

Taylor whipped her phone out and called 911.

The two of them worked together on getting Nia down from the ceiling. They laid her body on the floor. Nikki wrapped her arms around her daughter as she prayed to God that he would spare her daughter's life. She attempted to check her pulse but couldn't find it because she simply didn't know a thing about checking pulses. Taylor stood inches away from Nia, and she prayed hard and was still praying. Her face flooded with tears as she stared at Nia and had so many questions. Her main question was 'Why'? She didn't understand why would Nia try to take her own life. What could have transpired that was so bad that pushed her to her limits? She always thought of Nia as being a strong individual who never gave a fuck and could care less what a person thought of her or said about her. She just didn't understand and just wanted to know WHY!

CHAPTER 3

"OH JAKAI, I'M SORRY BABY! I'M SO SORRY!" Michelle screamed at top of her lungs.

She realized that she had made a mistake. Once she pulled that trigger and saw JaKai jumping in front of that bullet she wished that she could have reversed that bullet and placed it back into the barrel of the gun. She loved JaKai with every fiber of her being and would never do anything to take his life. Harm him, yes, but take his life... hell no!

Michelle frantically gazed around the room as she tried to figure out what to do. "JaKai!" She cried.

JaKai grabbed his chest. He truthfully didn't know where he was shot. He just knew that it hurt like hell. "Are you fucking crazy woman!" He managed to say.

Michelle batted her eyes and helped get him to the bed.

"Call 911. What the fuck are you sitting around crying for?" He asked with an attitude. He couldn't believe that Michelle had shot him and was sitting around crying and shit instead of getting him the medical attention he needed.

"Who was she? Do you love her?" Michelle found herself questioning.

JaKai was ready to have a fit. He couldn't believe the nerve of Michelle. "Bitch are you fucking
crazy! Get me some fucking help!" JaKai yelled.

Michelle thought about calling 911 then she thought about her going to jail. *'Crazy girlfriend shot boyfriend'* was the only thing that crossed her mind. She began freaking out. "JaKai we can't call 911." She said snatching up his phone up and hers. Then she ran into the bathroom and threw both phones in. Running back into the room, JaKai was lifting himself up from the bed. Michelle pushed his ass right back down, nudging him in his chest.

"Ahhh." JaKai grunted.

Michelle ran her hands over her disheveled hair. "It's all because of you JaKai! I can't and I won't go to jail," she cried.

"Bitch you are fucking selfish! This is why I cheat on your dumb ass!" JaKai groaned.

Any bitch that put anything before JaKai, in his eyes, was a goner. He couldn't stand motherfuckers like Michelle who always thought about themselves and no one else.

Michelle ran towards JaKai. She was all over the room and all over the place. Her brain wasn't settled. "What did you call me?" She yelled. She reached her hand and slapped him across the face.

He was vexed and had enough of her. Through the incredible amount of pain he was in he still managed to pounce on Michelle's ass. He knocked her right on the floor and climbed on top of her. SMACK! SMACK! AND SMACK AFTER SMACK! He smacked her across her face. She screamed, cried and pleaded in defense. She had really pushed JaKai to his limits and she didn't know if he was going to send her to meet her maker or just simply beat her ass senseless. When JaKai was done, he stood up with blood pouring from his wound, dick swinging and all. He stared at Michelle. She was nothing but trash in his eyes, just like her damn pathetic ass brother. The thought of her brother appeared across his mind. He hated that the motherfucker was still alive and fighting for his life. He should have ended it. He hated to be tested and out of all the motherfuckers in the world he felt like the two that tested him had connections, which was blood. Brother and sister. His dick stood salute as if his little head was thinking the same as his big head. He released his bladder all over Michelle who was now curled up in a ball. "You fucking bitch you could have killed me!" He spat. He grabbed his pants and rushed out the house.

Michelle jumped up as if that ass whipping wasn't enough for her and was right on his tail. Jotting down the steps, she pounced on his back. She was furious and it caused them both to fall to the ground. They tussled across the marble floor, and JaKai flipped her over on her back.

"Ahhh." Michelle cried when her frail body hit that marble floor. She ran towards their fire place and picked up a long, tall 3foot candle and hit him with it. Blood gushed from his head and a part of him was telling him that he should kill or be killed. Because the madness Michelle was filled with he just knew if he didn't fight her ass off he wasn't going to make it out of there alive.

JaKai threw her down on her back so damn hard that it knocked the wind out of her. She had to catch her breath. By the time she got up, he was in his car and flying away from her like a bat out of hell. He weaved in and out of the lanes when his vision had become blurry and he could feel his heart race beating now at a much slower pace. He felt like his life was slipping right out of his hands.

"FIGHT, JAKAI! FIGHT!" He coached himself. Putting his foot to the medal he drove faster. He grabbed his phone to call an ambulance and discovered it was dead. He thought it was the gun wound that was pushing him near death, but it wasn't. It was the powerful blow of the candle to his head.

He reached up to his rearview mirror and pushed the OnStar button. Connecting with the operator he could barely speak. "9-1-1!" He yelled.

The operator was on point when she quickly GPS-ed JaKai's car and his movement. "Please pull over Mr. House," she said. "Help is on it's way."

Before JaKai knew it, he lost control of the wheel. His body shook, which was soon discovered as a seizure. The car spun out of control, bearing off the side of the road. His head banged against the steering wheel. He was seconds away from death.

When he woke up, he was lying in a hospital bed with IV's in his arms and was stripped naked with nothing but a half of a night gown covering his body.

"Sir do you know where you are?" He was immediately asked.

JaKai squinted his eyes. "If it ain't heaven then I better be in a damn hospital." He said. He tried to move and raise his, but before he could even to do so another seizure took over his body. Doctors rushed in the room and instantly put JaKai in an induced coma.

CHAPTER 4

Michelle was furious. She ran into the kitchen and grabbed an oversized butcher's knife and thought about hunting JaKai down and slicing his ass up into a million of pieces. She calmed down a bit and thought for a split second. If she couldn't have JaKai then no one was going to have him. Just as she was about to place a call and get JaKai handled for once and for all her cellphone rung.

"Coming!" She screamed as if her caller could hear her. Her eyes scanned all around the house as she tried to figure out where she had her cellphone last. She began to tear up the house, throwing and tossing things all over the place. She ran upstairs and sighed when she found it sitting on the bed. "Hello." She huffed, picking the phone up. Seeing that it was Leo calling her she quickly changed her voice into a more mellow and softer tone. "Hey, Leo, baby I was just thinking about you." Pacing her bedroom floor she looked in the mirror and could barely stare at her reflection. Her cherubic face was all swollen and scratched up as if no one loved her. It hurt like hell the way JaKai did her. She should have killed him and the pretty thick bitch that he had hiding in her closet. Tears ran down her cheeks.

"Are you okay?" Leo asked, hearing Michelle's broken tone.

Michelle thought for a second then threw herself onto the bed. "No, Leo I'm not okay," she cried. "My drug dealing boyfriend just came home and beat the crap out of me. My face is all swollen up and I don't know what to do."

Leo he raised his eyebrows and had stopped doing what he was doing. "He did what?" Leo asked.

Michelle began to tell him the story piece by piece, excusing all of her actions and making up a lie to make herself look like the victim.

"Do you allow him to harbor drugs there Michelle?" he asked. "Please tell me you don't."

She sniffled. "I feel like such a fool. I've allowed him to. Please don't judge me."

"Who is your man if you don't mind me asking? You know how I feel about you. That nigga ain't going to get away with this shit."

She smiled. He was now on her side and that's all she needed. She sang like a bird, telling Leo any and everything he wanted to know about JaKai.

He then looked over at Streets who was standing next to him and nodded and gave him a thumbs up. Word on the streets was that JaKai and Luke were out there getting it. And Leo and his crew wanted a piece of the cake. With confirmation from Michelle they were going to get it.

Leo wanted that shit today. At that second greed took over him and it was time to make a move so that he could get caught up with all of his expenses and child support and get back on his feet. Hell he didn't give a damn if 50 bands was all got. He needed a come up and needed one quick.

"Baby hang tight. When I close shop I will hit you up." He told Michelle.

Little did she know, she would be seeing Leo a lot sooner than planned. She smiled and hung up the phone. She went to the shower and stepped in, thinking of JaKai— the things she was going to do to him— she was now his worst nightmare. She was going to make sure the rest of his life was a living hell. A devilish smile appeared on her face as she lathered the soap to wash her body.

She began humming tune of Mary J. Blige's "Not Gon' Cry" before she sang it aloud while trying not to shed a tear. Meanwhile her vocals reached their highest, and tears rolled down her cheeks, her eyes were closed tight and she was in a deep daze.

******

Outside of Michelle's house stood Streets and Leo. In broad daylight they were ready to get down with the get down. Streets and Leo had been boys for so long. They met about 6 years ago in jail when they both were doing hard time. Streets was doing a long bid and so was Leo. Ever since then they had been tight, having one another's back. Both were released from prison not too long ago and since then they both had been making moves and come ups. Robbing, stealing, killing and whatever they could get into to get that money. Leo was hustling hard doing what he had to do to keep his business up. Before he got busted he invested his drug money into a rim shop, trying to make an honest living. But then he got busted, and the girl who he thought had his back took him for everything he got. Had he not paid the shop up for years in advanced he would have lost that too. When he came home he was on the verge of losing his shop, he was homeless and the only shelter and source of income he had was his shop, which he couldn't lose. So he did what he had to do and that was getting it how he lived. When he met Michelle it was fate that brought the them together.

Nah, it was Streets! Streets was like a private investigator, tailing Michelle and stalking her ass for the past few weeks. Michelle was always calling Streets for shit to do. The last time he took care of business for her she tried to play him all the way to the left. He felt like so many times he would ask Michelle about leads on JaKai and for her to let him take care of him but she wouldn't allow him to do so; talking about she loved him and shit. But then when they weren't on good terms she would want Streets to do all types of bogus shit to JaKai. The last time when she didn't pay him and acted like he was some type of bitch was his last straw. He was now on a fuck JaKai and fuck Michelle level. He was trying to get money and the two of them had exactly what he wanted and more— what he needed in order to survive. Money was everything— the root of all evil, the cause of death, the key to living life.

Streets and Leo stood at the backdoor. Leo looked over at Streets. "Look, we only going in here to get the money and that's it. Nothing more, nothing less." Leo advised Streets who could, at times, get hot headed. He remembered the time the two of them decided to run insode a corner store. Streets' hot temper could have cost the both of them their lives. The nigga had no chill whatsoever.

"Nigga you ain't got to tell me shit," Streets said with an attitude. "This is my fucking blood. I ain't trying to hurt her, I'm just trying to get that dough."

"Then we shouldn't have any problems."

Streets agreed with him.

The two of them pulled black ski masks over their faces and were dressed in black attire from top to bottom, and even had the black gloves on to leave no finger prints behind.

Leo picked up a brick and was about to crack the glass to the back door until Streets turned the knob and discovered that the door was unlocked. The two just couldn't believe how much money JaKai was getting and how careless he was living or allowing his bitch to live. Because if any nigga wanted a motherfucker they knew the way to get to them was through their girl or through their immediate family.

"These motherfuckers stupid." Streets said before him and Leo burst into a light laughter then went back to business.

They walked into the house and locked the doors behind them. The two of them separated going through the kitchen, with one going left and the other to the right. After thoroughly searching the kitchen they met up in the living room. Leo went to the front door and locked it.

Their ears were filled with a high-pitched cry. Atlas they thought it was but it was really Michelle singing her little heart out.

"Let's hurry and get what we came for and bounce." Streets said.

They walked up the steps and went their separate ways of searching the upstairs. The coast was clear and there wasn't a soul in site but Michelle's loud ass who was in the shower.

Streets went to stand at the bathroom door while Leo tore the bedroom up. When he found the big safe in the closet his eyes lit up. 'JACKPOT!' He thought. Learning Michelle over the past few weeks and listening to everything she had told him he tried to place the numbers to the safe but couldn't get it if his life depended on it. He became furious. He rushed back out the room and met with Streets at the bathroom door. "I can't crack that motherfucker." He said.

Before Streets could say anything, Leo snatched the bathroom door wide open.

Startling the hell out of Michelle, she thought it was JaKai coming back for her but was even more scared when she saw the two masked men standing before her. Her heart fell to the bottom of her stomach. While standing in the shower scared shitless she pissed all over herself. "PLEASE! WHAT ARE YOU HERE FOR?" Michelle cried.

Leo yanked her out the shower by her arms. "Bitch, where is the fucking money." He said with a muffled voice. He slung Michelle's bony ass out the bathroom. Her wet body fell on the floor and damn near slid down the hallway. He walked to her and yoked her up by her hair.

"AHHH!" Michelle cried.

Leo led her into the bedroom, to the closet where the safe was located. "OPEN THIS SHIT!" He demanded.

Michelle batted her eyes. Her chest was heaving up and down at a weird pace. She looked at Leo and was about to say something until Streets whipped the gun out and pointed it towards her head. "There's nothing here. My boyfriend took everything!"

Leo wasn't hearing that shit because that sure as hell wasn't the story that Michelle was just singing to him minutes ago.

She slowly began to punch the keys in the safe. Her mind was all over the place, plus she was so damn scared that she couldn't punch in the correct code to the safe.

Streets lifted the gun and knocked Michelle in the head with the butt of the gun.

"PLEAESEEEEE!" Michelle cried grabbing her head. She finally entered the correct code and the safe swung open.

Streets and Leo's eyes widened.... in pure disappointment!

"Where is the fucking money!" Streets roared.

Michelle was in pain from the bashing upside her head with the gun, plus the whipping JaKai had put on her minutes ago that she couldn't even pick up her own cousin's voice. "We don't have any fucking money! He took the shit!"

Streets was furious. Before he knew it he was snapping out on Michelle. He lifted her little body up from the ground and slung her across the room like a rag doll. Rushing over towards her he towered over her small body and beat.

Leo rushed to him and stopped him from taking Michelle's life.

Michelle balled her body up tightly and cried her eyes out. She couldn't believe all this horrible shit was happening to her and happening to her so damn quickly. Trouble after trouble, heartache after heartache. She didn't know what the fuck to do. At the moment she gave up and she didn't care if the masked men would have beaten her to death.

The drama between her and JaKai— her man who she shot. His cheating and lying ass. His young out of control side chicks, the drama that popped off with her parents, the terrible situation that Michael was in. All of it was just too much for her. So damn overwhelming that she just wanted to give up.

Leaving out Leo saw Michelle's purse resting on the bed. He yanked it up, going through it. Seeing a book of checks in there he was well satisfied. Then he snatched her cellphone.

"JUST TAKE EVERYTHING!" Michelle cried. She didn't have to tell them twice. That's exactly what they were going to do. Take every damn thing to her name and then some if she had that to offer.

The two of them walked down the steps and out the house like nothing had happened. Walking to the car, Streets was mad as fuck. "I could have killed that bitch." He sneered.

Leo shook his head before they got into the car. He waived the check book. "Let's make this shit do what it do." He said.

Streets grabbed the check book. "I hope that bitch got something up in that damn account."

Leo laughed. "I don't know how much, but something is in there. Why the fuck else would she be walking around with a damn check book." He shook his head and started the ignition.

Streets nodded. Leo was clearly speaking sense to him.

He knew the perfect chick who would go and bust the checks for them. He was hoping he would make some sort of come up off it. With Michelle's driver's licenses, cellphone and other proof of identity in her purse that's all he needed. Leo headed into the direction of Northeast DC to one of his old homie's crib.

CHAPTER 5

When JaKai woke up, he was in an incredible amount of pain. He gazed around the room and realized that he was still in the hospital, hooked up to the numerous machines that was making loud beeping noises that was driving him insane. When he tried to move, the terrible pain in his left side reminded him that he was shot. The thought of Michelle crossed his mind. He couldn't wait until he was released from the hospital so he could beat the shit out of her. Nia crossed his mind then and he laughed at the thought of Nia going crazy from not being able to get ahold of him all day. He reached for the phone and began to punch Nia's number in. When not being able to get her correct number he gave up and tossed the phone to the side. "Ahhhh!" He grunted trying to prop himself up. Just as he was struggling trying to lift himself up, two undercover detectives walked into the room. JaKai shook his head. He couldn't stand them fucking boys better known as damn pigs. "What the fuck you two motherfuckers want?" He spat.

The officers looked at one another and stepped into the room. "We ain't here for that bullshit," the black officer said. "All we want to know is one thing. Who shot you, brother?"

JaKai burst into laughter. Then he thought about it. Vindictiveness was embedded in his mind. If he went and served Michelle the ass whipping she'd been dying for him to give her... She'd been doing all types of outrageous shit to get his attention and now she had it. He weighed his options. If he would give Michelle exactly what she wanted he would possibly end up in jail. So he played the games that she loved to play. Now that it was two playing the same game she wouldn't like that shit. Giving Michelle a taste of her own medicine he cracked a smile. "My crazy ass ex-girlfriend tried to kill me and I want to press charges. She shot me then she beat me and threatened to take my life."

Both officers looked at one another and laughed. They couldn't believe that JaKai was being serious. They waited to see if he was joking, but seeing the seriousness on his face they had no choice but to take out their pens and pads and get JaKai's story. After hearing enough, they figured they didn't come to the hospital for nothing. So they sided with JaKai, charing Michelle with 1st degree assault, attempt murder, domestic violence and a gang of other charges.

JaKai watched them walk out the door with a satisfied look on his face. He struggled reaching over to grab the ice chips that rested in a plastic cup. He grabbed a few and sat back to chug them and laughed to himself. PAY BACK WAS A BITCH!

CHAPTER 6

Nikki and Taylor stood beside Nia's bed. Nikki couldn't stop thanking the doctors and God for sparing her child's life. She couldn't remember the last time she prayed. But that very day she utilized prayer so much that one would have thought she was in church religiously or at least read the bible on the daily. She couldn't tell anyone the last time she read the bible if she was asked. Hell she didn't even own a bible and probably couldn't have pointed one out. But that day she knew what people meant when they said it was 'power in prayer.' Because she prayed, prayed, prayed and prayed and now her daughter was stablw and breathing on her own, all thanks and praises went to the man upstairs. Nikki didn't know what she would have done if Nia didn't make it. Had her daughter died, someone was going to prepare a double casket and funeral because she wasn't going to stay on earth without her daughter. Although Nikki and Nia had a strange kind of relationship, they were like best friends and loved one another with every fiber of their being. Nikki promised herself from that day forward she was going to be the best mother she could be to Nia and change everything that was in her control to change. There was going to be no more letting Nia do what she wanted and how she pleased. No more acting like her best friend instead of her mother. None of that nonsense in their home. Nikki promised she was going to get a good job where she could provide for Nia, but not work too many hours that prohibited her from being a mother as well.

She rubbed her fingers across Nia's hands while Nia got all the rest she could. Nia's body had been through an incredible amount of pain and the only thing that could heal her besides prayer was rest.

"Wake up baby girl," Nikki whispered softly into Nia's ear, tickling the little hairs inside.

Nia could hear Nikki clearly but decided to play possum as long as she could. She wasn't ready to face the music just yet.

Taylor sat in the chair beside the bed with tears on her cheeks. She was staring at Nia, lying there, so hard she could really pierce a hole in Nia's soul. Taylor's mind was all over the place. She was happy that Nia was now alive but upset that her best and only friend tried to leave her the way she did. Without warning her or talking to her. Taylor cellphone rang and she noticed that it was her parents. It made her more moody that she turned it off and huffed. "I wish these motherfuckers would just let me be." She said folding her arms across her chest.

Nikki kept on shaking Nia, playing in her hair, rubbing her hands across her face and all types of shit, irritating Nia's soul until she had gotten tired of playing possum. Nia squinted her eyes. "Momma." She said with a soft hoarse voice.

Nikki's eyes widened. "Baby! Yes it's momma!" Nikki yelled excitedly.

Nia cringed. "Damn, Nikki why you got to be so loud?"

Taylor stood up and approached the bed. "Nia." She said in a soft tone.

Nia turned her head to look at Taylor and their eyes locked and words were exchanged with their eyes only.

Taylor broke down crying. She covered her mouth and ran out of the room. She couldn't hold it in anymore. She couldn't differentiate if it was her pregnancy or if she was just simply mad at what Nia had done. Either way she was beyond hurt. She didn't know what she would do without her best friend. She was running down the hallway when she heard her name being called and stopped. She turned around to follow the call of her name to see who it could've been. She poked her head inside the room "JaKai?" She raised her eyebrows when seeing him propped up in the bed with his legs kicked up while eating ice chips. She walked further into the room and closed the door behind her.

JaKai beckoned for her to come closer to him. Taylor walked over to him, staring at him like she had seen a ghost. "What the fuck are you looking at me like that for girl? Are you okay?" JaKai laughed.

Taylor shook her head and wrapped her arms around him. "Damn, I thought that girl killed you." She admitted.

"Ahhh!" JaKai grunted pushing her off of him. "Nah shorty, real soldiers don't die."

Taylor waved him off and wiped her eyes. "Boy please."

JaKai grabbed her hand. "What the fuck was you crying for? You thought a nigga was dead? You crying over me?"

Taylor laughed at him. "Don't flatter yourself."

He then grabbed her by her arm with a smile on his face. "Come sit on daddy and lets finish what we started today." He looked down at his little man who was waking up already, anticipating on some good old action.

Taylor grinned and thought about it. Since she had become pregnant she was a horn dog.

He grabbed her hand tightly and damn near forced her upon him.

Taylor jumped on his lap and he tore at her shirt. He couldn't wait to get a taste of her sweet nipples. He thought about dipping his head between her sugar walls. He didn't give a fuck if he was laid up in the hospital, shot up and beat up, he wanted some pussy and wanted it badly.

"Sit on my face now!" He told Taylor.

Taylor began to climb up on his face until she thought about Nia— her best friend who was just fought a terrible battle. She felt guilty and climbed off of his lap. She knew how Nia felt about JaKai and with her sneaking around with him made her nothing more than a back stabbing, trifling ass bitch. Then she thought about Luke. She cared about him. Even worse she was carrying his child and she knew Luke had so much love for her. Not to mention she could have lost her life fucking with JaKai. He wasn't worth it and the sex sure as hell wasn't worth losing Luke over. Besides, Luke's dick was even better and he loved Taylor even harder.

"JaKai we need to stop this shit right now," she told him. "I almost died fucking with you. Hell you almost got killed fucking with me. Don't you think enough is enough?" She then pulled up a chair and sat in it.

He frowned. "Man come on. You got me all hard and shit. Don't do this shit right now."

She shook her head. "Niggas like you always thinking with your dick. That's your downfall. Can't you see that shit?"

He wasn't trying to see shit at that moment but Taylor's juicy thighs wrapped around his head as he ate her pussy.

"Nia loves the shit out of you, and Luke loves you like a brother, and he really cares about me. We can't continue to hurt the people we love and who loves us over some good sex. There ain't nothing between us and nor will there ever be."

JaKai shook his head, now coming to his senses. "Where is Nia's ass anyways?"

Taylor swallowed the lump in her throat. The tears she couldn't fight back resurfaced, and it made JaKai raise his eyebrows and look at her like she was crazy. A bad feeling overcame him. "Where the fuck is she?" JaKai damn near yelled, forcing himself to sit up in his bed.

Taylor bit her lip. "She's a few rooms down from you. SHE TRIED TO KILL HERSELF! IT WAS FUCKING HORRIBLE. HER MOTHER AND I WENT TO HER HOUSE AND SHE WAS HANGING FROM THE CEILING!"

His jaw dropped. He couldn't believe the shit that was coming from Taylor's mouth. At that moment he realized he cared for Nia more than he cared for Taylor. Truth to be told he loved Nia and was heartbroken when Taylor told him what had happened. "Get me the fuck up out of here and take me to her now." JaKai ordered. He paged the nurses and demanded a wheelchair. Minutes later the nurse and Taylor helped JaKai to get settled in the wheelchair.

Taylor leaned forward to JaKai. "Remember this shit between us ends today," she said, pulling her pinky in front of him. "The shit never happened."

JaKai nodded and wrapped his pinky around hers for a pinky swear. "Right. I was never in that good ass pussy."

Taylor nudged him softly in the back of his head. "I swear you make me sick!" She laughed.

The two of them gave playfully remarks to one another while Taylor wheeled him to Nia's room where she stopped and took a deep breath. She mentally had to prepare herself before seeing Nia's face again. She was still upset with her.

They opened the door and walked in. Nia turned to face them. When she saw JaKai she was highly upset to the point where her blood pressure was rising and her blood was boiling. JaKai pushed her over the edge. All her life she wanted to be loved and when she found it he shat on her, or so she thought. She didn't know that it wasn't JaKai who was texting her and that it was Michelle. She was furious again when she thought about the fake Facebook page that had ruined her life. She could never return to that school again with all the shit that people saw. A video of her fucking, sucking and getting fucked— a young girl's worst nightmare.

"GET HIM OUT OF HERE!" Nia screamed.

JaKai was taken aback by the way Nia was yelling and carrying on. She was always happy to see him. The hurt look painted on her face was telling him something else. "What you talking about lil butt?" JaKai laughed.

"I HATE YOU! I DON'T EVER WANT TO SEE YOU AGAIN!"

Nikki stood up and furiously spat, "Taylor get him out of here! He's upsetting my daughter!"

Taylor looked at JaKai then at Nia. "What did he do to you Nia?" she asked. "He's been asking about you."

Nia rolled her eyes. "What didn't he do to me?" She bit her bottom lip and began playing with her fingers. He had her head over heels for him, loving him hard and hating him all at the same time. Just his presence alone was driving her insane. She literally wanted to hop across that bed, hop on JaKai's lap and give him the business.

"Mannn Nia tripping," he said to Taylor. "Take me back to my fucking room."

Taylor gazed at Nia who nodded her head. She bit her lip and stared at their backside with so many questions that she wanted to ask JaKai. The same question that everyone wanted to ask her. Why?

"Wait!" She screamed. "JaKai we really need to talk. Like right now."

Taylor stopped in her tracks and turned JaKai around.

Nikki huffed and threw her arms across her chest, now wearing a mean mug on her face.

"Can you bring him over here?" Nia asked Taylor.

Taylor did as she was asked. She looked Nia up and down. "And Nia we need to talk too."

Nia nodded. "Can you two please give JaKai and I five minutes. Then I want to talk to the both of you."

"Okay." Taylor softly said.

"Hmmm," Nikki hummed. "You better not hurt my daughter again or that's your fucking ass." She said to JaKai, purposely brushing against him as she walked past.

The two of them walked out the door, closing it behind them. They stood behind it with their ears against as if they could really hear something behind that thick wood.

JaKai and Nia were silent and the tension in the room was so thick that it could've to been cut with a saw.

"What's up?" JaKai broke the ice.

Nia couldn't even look at him. She was so devastated, hurt, and heart filled with pain. Her heart began to race and tears welled up in her eyes and uncontrollably fell down her cheeks. "JaKai." She held her hand up, signaling him to give her a second.

"Where the fuck you want me to go? I'm not in the predicament to walk!" He shouted wheeling himself closer to Nia.

"Why did you do this to me? What about all of the stuff you said to me? All of that shit was nothing to you but meant everything to me!"

He squinted his eyes. He was so damn confused that he didn't know where Nia was coming from. "I'm not perfect but I try my best. You know I had a girl at home. The bitch shot me because Luke, Taylor and I went over to the house to get the rest of my shit," he said half-honestly. "Luke had an emergency and Taylor was upstairs in the closet. I was in the bathroom. I came in when I heard the two of them arguing. She pulled the gun out on Taylor and I jumped in front of it. I was leaving her because a nigga ain't feeling her but feeling some little young shorty with a lil' butt." He smiled.

Nia started to smile but then the text messages he had sent her still needed to be explained. "Why did you text me all of that stuff?"

JaKai looked at her. "I ain't text you nothing girl! I don't even have your number anymore." Wheeling himself closer to Nia he handed his phone over to her after he found it.

Nia looked at his phone and could tell that it was fairly new. Still she went into his messages and noticed that he didn't have not one number stored. She shook her head as she reached for her phone and gave it to him.

He went through her messages and saw the shit that was sent to her. "Oh nah baby, that bitch went and got a new phone and texted you this shit. You know I don't even talk like that. And what the fuck you mean? I'm a daddy?" he then said proudly.

Nia covered her face and sighed, and tears began rolling down her cheeks again. "It's all bad. I'm only in here because I lost control of my life. I tried to kill the baby, then myself."

With all the strength in him, JaKai lifted himself out the wheelchair and sat in the tiny empty space that was next to Nia. He grabbed her by her face. "You tried to do what?" He said through gritted teeth, forcing Nia to look deep into his eyes.

"Kill me and the baby." She told him again.

JaKai was furious and beyond hurt, but at the same time he wanted to be there for Nia. He didn't know exactly what was going on but he had a question and he wanted a damn answer to it. "Why the fuck you try to do that? I should fucking choke the life out of you for trying to get rid of my seed without fucking talking to me first!" He said banging his fist against the side railing of the bed.

She looked up at the hurt in his eyes. "I'm sorry Kai," was all she was able to say.

"No tell me why the fuck you being so fucking selfish girl!"

She handed him her phone. "When I texted you, you told me you didn't want nothing to do with the baby and that it wasn't yours, to get rid of it. I haven't heard from you since. I made an appointment to get an abortion but the scheduling was way too far away. So I decided to wait it out. I go to school the next day to see this," she said helping him find the video and the fake Facebook page.

JaKai looked at the video and shook his head. He narrowed the eyes when he realized the views of the video was in the millions and the following was well over 2 million.

"I was devastated. I only recorded you and I to get back at your girlfriend, in case it got cute. She sent me photos of the two of you naked together in bed and I sent her the video. That's how all this started. She made a fake Facebook page, added damn near my entire school and posted this video.

After arriving at school and seeing this shit, it pushed me over the edge. I lost control." She began crying again.

JaKai was pissed. He couldn't wait to get his hands on Michelle. When he got ahold of her ass he was going to ring her by her fucking neck. He couldn't believe how low down and dirty her ass was.

JaKai wrapped his arms around Nia. He felt so bad for her. He began brushing her hair with his fingers. "Is my child okay?" He asked.

Nia nodded. "But my coochie hurts!" She blurted.

"Daddy going to fix that later." He curled his lips up and squeezed her tighter. "I love you. I love both of you and your ass better fucking protect my child."

"Wait, did you tell me you love me?" She was shocked.

JaKai grabbed her chin and looked deep into her eyes. "I love you Nia and my unborn, and we are going to be good."

Nia laid her head on his chest. "Damn boy! I love you too!"

The two of them cuddled while lost in their own thoughts. Nia was finally happy and was hoping she could move on with her life with JaKai. JaKai on the other hand was thinking about making major moves to be able to put Nia in a nice ass home, get her a car and do all he could do for his unborn child. He couldn't believe that he was about to be a father! He had forgotten all about Michelle telling him that she was pregnant when the fight broke out between Taylor and her. Truth to be told he could care less about Michelle's crazy ass.

A few minutes later Taylor walked into the room and Nia looked up. "JaKai, let me holla at my girl for a second." She told him.

He nodded and rubbed Nia's stomach and kissed her on the forehead.

Taylor folded her arms while she watched JaKai struggle to get back in the wheelchair. She threw her hands down to her side. "Ya'll both are all fucked up!" She said, walking over to JaKai and helping him back in the wheelchair. They all laughed at her comment. She then wheeled JaKai outside of the door. "What's up?" Taylor asked Nia, pulling up a chair and sitting beside her bed.

Nia balled her lips. Her eyes began to blink, fighting back the tears. The look on Taylor's face did it all. She hated to see her girl hurt or upset. Especially with her being the cause of it. "I'm sorry Taylor." She said lowly.

"Sorry for what?" Taylor snapped. "That you tried to X yourself out of this world? That you didn't think about me! That you didn't even let me know what the fuck is going on?"

Nia shook her head and handed Taylor her cellphone. Every time Nia saw that Facebook page she wanted to lose it all over again.

Taylor looked at the video in disbelief. She was a bit jealous when she saw the way JaKai was eating her pussy and dicking her down like he was a damn hired pipe layer. That nigga was really laying some serious dick in that video. Taylor couldn't take it anymore. She handed the phone back to Nia, now understanding everything. "I'ma fucking kill that crazy ass bitch!" Taylor said through closed teeth. She then got out of her chair and wrapped her arms around Nia.

"I'm so sorry you have to go through this."

"I wish you would have come and talked to me, Nia. I swear, we would have faced that shit together then went and beat the life out of that bitch!" Taylor said balling her fist up.

Nia stared at her friend who was pissed the fuck off. "You mad shorty? My little pit bull in a skirt, someone brought the killa out in her." She laughed.

Taylor playfully nudged her. "Is there anything else you have to tell me?"

Nia smiled and rubbed her stomach. "Guess our kids are going to be born around the same time because I'm pregnant."

Taylor hugged her. “My parents are going to fucking kill me.” She replied.

“I know. What are you going to do?” Nia shook her head.

“I’ma go live with Luke. He went us both there with him.”

“Oh you told him?” Nia raised her eyebrow.

“I had no choice but too. I thought it was fair for him to know. Does your mother know yet?”

“She may have the idea, but she doesn’t know everything. So with that being said, go and grab her so I can fill her in.” Nia said, grabbing a cup of water and taking a sip from it.

Taylor watched as Nia sip the water, and around her neck was a bruise that had been swollen from all the pressure and the tightness from the rope that was recently wrapped around it. Taylor closed her eyes and quickly thanked God for sparing her best friend and for giving her a second shot at life, then on top of that for saving her child. Nia ruptured her insides by scrapping the wall with the hanger, but thankfully she didn’t kill her own child. Taylor believed in the power of prayer and God. Her parents were very religious, and now for the very first time she saw with her own eyes how God worked miracles.

“I love you.” The both said in unison and laughed at one another for doing so. They had been around one another for so long that they were just alike.

Taylor got up and began walking out the door.

“Oh and do you have something you have to tell me?” Nia exclaimed.

Taylor stood frozen. *Shit, what the fuck did JaKai tell her?* She began thinking. Her heart began running a marathon race. It was beating so fast that she thought it was about to fall out of her chest. She was about to have a panic attack and break down and cry. Instead, she turned around, wiping the worried look clear off her face. “Like what?” She raised her eyebrow.

"About JaKai and his girlfriend catching you in the closet."

SHIT! SHIT! FUCK! FUCK! Taylor thought. She narrowed her eyes at Nia. She was about to tell the truth.

"Girl I can't believe that bitch had the nerve to show out on you like that and all you were doing was helping JaKai get rest of his stuff." Nia spat, shaking her head.

Taylor sighed within.

"Luke should have never left you there knowing how that crazy bitch was. She could have killed you up in there! Insecure ass bitch!" Nia said grabbing her cup of water and sipped it again.

Taylor shook her head. She was thankful that JaKai covered up their mess completely. She was so not ready to face the music yet. "Man that girl is crazy. She must have thought I was you because she accused me of fucking him and some more shit."

"Mmm mm hmm, crazy ass hoe."

Taylor turned back around and went to go get Nikki. She found Nikki in the hallway flirting with an older Caucasian man. "Nikki, Nia want you." Taylor called after her.

Nikki turned around and gave the man a tight hug, brushing her breast against his chest. He watched her ass as she swayed her hips, making her way back over to Taylor. "That nigga got money." Nikki said.

Taylor shook her head at Nikki. She couldn't believe that Nikki didn't know the meaning of acting civilized. Here her daughter was laid up in the hospital and there Nikki was doing what she did best. Find a man that could take care of her and what she needed taken care of. Never knew how to separate the two from her responsibilities and her normal life.

Nikki smiled grabbing the handle to the room door. "Hell this is my life. Don't be looking at me, judging me and shit," she said.

Taylor smiled. "Judge free zone here, Nikki. I'm not my parents."

Nikki blew her a kiss then disappeared into the room. She sat on the edge of the bed and waited for Nia to begin talking.

Hearing her daughter and the way she wasn't there mentally for her, she was seconds away from breaking down and crying. Then going to go find Michelle and literally rip her heart out of her chest. Instead she fought back the tears and began to silently plan the torture she had in store for Michelle.

"Don't NO GROWN ASS WOMAN FUCK WITH MY CHILD!" Nikki told Nia. "And secondly, don't you ever hide anything like this from me again. I love you to death. You are the best of me— my better half! I know at times I can get out of control and be more of a friend to you than I should be. But don't you ever forget Nia, I'm your damn mother and you can come to me for anything. We don't make no weak motherfuckers in our family so don't start being one. Your ass was out here acting grown, so from here and out woman up to these grown woman duties that you are taking on. Do you hear me?"

Nia nodded. "Yes," was all she was able to say.

Michelle got up and hugged her daughter tightly. She then sat back in her chair and began plotting. If she couldn't get her hands on Michelle then she was going to get her hands on the next relations to her. She didn't give a damn who it was, but someone in that family was going to meet the grim reaper that was vicious and hidden within her being. Who Michelle now brought to life.

Visits where going to be made and repercussions were going to be paid...

CHAPTER 7

Luke had stepped out of the room away from his sister and mother, and took and made a few business calls. He looked down the hallway and thought he saw Taylor. He blinked and began walking towards the person who he thought was her. Standing behind her he knew it was her. He wrapped his arms around her, catching Taylor off guard. She turned around so hard that she could have broken her hip.

"Luke." She cooed.

"What are you doing here?" He asked.

"I was about to ask you that same question." Taylor sighed. "I'm here for many reasons. First you shouldn't have left me there with JaKai!"

Luke squinted his eyes. That was on his mind heavily. He knew that JaKai was a dog and was hoping that he was able to trust the two of them alone. "Why is that?" he asked.

Taylor shook her head. "I was in the closet helping him get some of his clothing and he was I don't even know where in the house, and before I knew it some crazy ass girl came in there and started snapping on me. Talking about I'm fucking JaKai and carrying his child and some more. Before I knew it, the girl pulled out a gun, JaKai come running in the room and she shot him!"

Luke stared into her eyes and believed every word she was saying. He was slowly but surely becoming a fool for Taylor. A fool for love. It wasn't a question if it could be love or not. It was love for sure. For the love of Taylor at that. Luke thought about Michelle and everything that Taylor was telling him sure as hell was adding up because that all sounded like her. But he had one question. "How did she know you was pregnant?" He asked.

"She didn't know I was pregnant. She thought I was Nia."

He was so damn lost. "So what the fuck she mean by being pregnant is what I'm asking."

Taylor sensed Luke had a bit of an attitude and didn't like it one bit. "She thought I was Nia, Luke! Nia is pregnant and some shit happened with her and Michelle. Michelle made a fake Facebook page and posted a video of JaKai and Nia having sex and posted it all over the internet. It has over 2 million followers. The shit is crazy. Nia got upset and tried to commit suicide."

All of it was too much drama for his liking. He was a get money on the low and mind his own business type of nigga. The tea was too damn hot for him and he didn't want to sip any of it. Every time he turned around Michelle's name was brought up into something. He was praying that JaKai was done with that crazy ass bitch. He couldn't wait until the day she tried to spill the beans about sucking Luke's dick. Which he doubted she would because that would just make her look even more like the whore she really was.

"I'ma kill that bitch for trying to do any harm to my girl and my child." Luke told Taylor. He then poked his head in at Nia and spoke to her for a brief second.

They walked hand in hand to JaKai's room. Luke got a similar story from JaKai which Taylor had told him. So he had no need in thinking that she was telling him any lies.

"Nigga I hope you are done with her for good." Luke said to JaKai.

"Man fuck that bitch!" he laughed. "I'm done with her ass, and call me petty but that bitch going to jail! I pressed all types of charges against that crazy ass bitch. The fuck she thought she was playing with. She better hope them blue and whites pick her ass up before I get ahold of her."

"Nah bruh, she better hope they get ahold of her before I get ahold of her crazy ass." Luke corrected JaKai. Because if he had gotten ahold of Michelle first it sure as hell wasn't going to be pretty. Luke turned to Taylor. “Come on. I got someone I want you to meet.” He said to Taylor. “I’ma be back to check you in a few.” He said to JaKai. Luke felt that it was time for Taylor to meet the lady of his life, so he took her back to Alesha’s room and introduced Taylor to his mother.

CHAPTER 8

Streets and Leo patiently waited outside of the bank while the young chick they picked up went in to cash some of the checks. They wrote two checks out for $8,500 and another for $9,500. Streets sat in the passenger, biting his nails as his mind wandered back to Alesha. Little did she know she really broke his heart. There wasn't a day that went by that he didn't think about her. He wished he knew more about her. Especially like where she lived. Had he known a physical address he would have been stalking her and forced her into being with him. He understood that she was young and didn't want to get him or herself into any trouble, but he didn't give a fuck about that. He needed and wanted her. The day she came into his life, he been happy. The day she left, he became miserable. He wasn't going to give up on her. He knew it was their destiny to be with one another. Besides that, he was so damn nervous and hungry. For that money that was.

Leo on the other hand was busy plotting on their next lick. If this shit didn't work out, then he was going after one of these big time balling ass niggas on the street. He had heard so much about Luke and he wanted a piece of that pie. He remembered Luke from back in the day when they used to stand on the same block together. He knew way back then that Luke had potential and that it was a possibility of him making it. Being that Luke was always the first one on the block, beating the sun in the morning, and the last one out on the block, he was faithful to his grind and had put so much muscle into his hustle. "This bitch better make something shake." Leo said to Streets.

Streets nodded.

Minutes later a young girl wearing her hair slicked back into a ponytail, gold studs resting in her ear lobes, a black pair of slacks, soft pink tank top underneath with a black blazer atop of it made her way to the car. Her pumps clicked against the pavement. She gripped her clutch tighter and reached for the door handle to get in the backseat. Trying to open the door she realized that it was locked. "Let me in." She spoke in a soft voice.

Leo started the car up. "Do you have my fucking money Monica." He snapped.

She reached in the window and unlocked the door herself. She threw her clutch down in the backseat and pulled out a cigarette and lit it up. Blowing smoke into the air she mean mugged Leo.

"Do you have my fucking money?" He barked turning around in the driver's seat.

Monica squinted her eyes at him and blew smoke in his direction. "What type of shit do you have me into?" Monica nonchalantly asked. She haven't been back in a town for a year and already she was into some shit. Her plans were to come back in town in silence, find Luke and hopefully win his heart over again. She knew she fucked up when she left Luke and aborted his child, she was still kicking herself in the ass for that. She got with her so called doctor of hers and found her he was nothing more than a street pharmacist, two and a half years later and two kids, he ended up getting booked. Crushing all her long terms dreams. Now she was back at what she knew best again.

Leo snatched up her clutch. Opening it he saw the swollen envelopes inside of it. He looked back at Monica and smiled before snatching the money up out of it. "This bitch is fucking bad!" He high fived Streets. Then he smelled the money and began counting it.

"Nigga pull the fuck off!" Streets said.

Leo pulled out of the parking lot. He passed the money to Streets and Streets counted it. He pulled off a stack to be exact and threw it to Monica. She kindly accepted the money and tucked it into her bra along with the other $7,000 check she had stolen from them and cashed as well. She didn't know what the fuck Streets and Leo was into but she didn't give a damn, as long as they kept the money flowing. She had plans for the two funny acting ass motherfuckers. She was going to cash all the checks they gave her and then later take what the fuck she cashed from them. She might have had habits on the side, been a fool before, but today was a new day and she was no longer a fool. She was that bitch that no one thought she could be.

They took Monica all across DC, robbing Michelle blind by cashing checks, to two other Bank Of Americas and three check cashing places. By the end of the day they had a total of $90,000 in their pockets and Monica had $10,000, so they thought. Not including the $20,000 in checks she had cashed on her own.

"This is that shit I'm talking about!" Leo exclaimed.

Streets nodded. He didn't feel bad at all for stealing from his own blood.

Leo looked over at Streets. "Call that bitch up and see what she talking about."

"Nigga we got her phone," he said. "Why don't you make a pop up to her place and see what's up with her. See if that bitch got more money."

Leo nodded. Tonight he was going to splurge a little bit, flip some money and the next day he would stop by and check on Michelle. He drove down to the Monaco hotel where he rented a suite for $750 a night. It was something that he always wanted to treat himself to. The threesome got out of the car like Bonnie, Clyde and the sidekick and headed into the hotel.

"Ya'll boys are about that money!" Monica said to them as they all got on the elevator.

"Bitch and you know that." Streets said to her.

She turned her nose up and ignored his smart remark. All that day he was snapping back at her like he knew who the fuck she was or something and she didn't like one bit of that. Instead she ignored him and turned the other cheek.

Once they got settle into the room, Leo called up his pill man, coke man and weed man and ordered a party pack for the three of them to get their life that night.

Later the three of them was at the stadium turning up like a motherfucker, spending hella cash. When they left, Monica had to help carry Leo and Streets out to the car. After securing them into the backseat she pulled off and drove them back to their hotel. Her plans were all out of whack. She didn't plan on getting as drunk as she did. But with all the free alcohol, coke, Mollys and other free shit she couldn't turn down or say no even if her life depended on it. So she lived in the moment and partied like a true Rockstar. When they got back to the room, Monica helped Leo get into one bed and Streets into the other. She had decided to either sleep with Leo's fine ass or on the couch. The last time Leo fucked her, he fucked her so damn good that she was begging for his last name. That shit was like crack. She got one hit and wanted more. His head game was on point and his big thick dick could literally knock walls down. Monica eased out the shower wearing nothing at all. She went into Leo's pocket and pulled out the clear baggie filled with coke. She bumped a few lines and then slid into the bed with him. His dick was already on hard. She eased under the covers and wrapped her warm mouth around his thick shaft.

The warmth of her mouth woke Leo out of his drunken sleep. He grabbed Monica by her head and ran his fingers through her soft hair. "MMMM… OHHH SHIT." He moaned.

Monica lifted her head and spat on his dick while stroking it.

Leo found her wet pussy underneath the covers and started massaging her it with his fingers. Monica came up from the covers and lay on top of them to spread her legs in a V shape. Leo thought about it. He never ate her pussy before but her freshly shaven kitty was calling his name. He flicked his tongue against her while shoving three fingers inside of her vagina. Her walls tightly wrapped around them.

"Ohhhh Leo." She cooed while squeezing her breast. She threw her head back and closed her eyes as she enjoyed the ecstasy of him eating her.

Streets woke up out of his sleep and was in the other bed stroking his manhood underneath the covers. He was so damn horny that he didn't know what the hell to do. He eased out of the bed and approached Leo from behind. He had heard many rumors on the streets and in jail that Leo was a little sweet. Tonight he tried his charm and just as he guessed, Leo was as sweet as they came. He shoved Leo's oversized dick into his mouth, and seconds later he had him moaning and groaning. The best head Leo had ever gotten was from a man!

Monica opened her eyes at all the moaning. She turned her head to the bed where Streets was sleeping and couldn't believe the nigga had woken up and was no longer there. Her eyes widen at the site of Streets sucking the life out of Leo's dick. In her twenty-three years of living she had never seen such trifling shit. She was ready to vomit and cum at the same time. She held the vomit and came all over Leo's face.

Minutes later she was witnessing these two wannabe tough men fucking each other. Monica slid out of the bed and grabbed Leo's pants. She crawled across the floor and opened the safe. She took all of the money out of it and filled it into her clutch. She grabbed Streets shirt and placed it over her body. She looked back at them as the two of them engaged in a 69 position. She eased the car keys out of her purse and crawled back on the floor and got Streets and Leo's cellphones, wallets and random shit in their pockets. Standing up at the door she cracked it open just a bit. She pulled out her phone and snapped a picture. The light from her camera startled the two of them. Both gay motherfuckers were caught in action.

"YAL FAGGOT ASS NIGGAS!" Monica screamed and turned around to get ghost.

Leo jumped up and saw that the safe was open. Naked, he and Streets both ran out the hotel room chasing after Monica.

She was already on the elevator pushing the L on the panel for the Lobby. Just as Leo hit the elevator he tried to jam the door open. Streets took the emergency steps down. Monica got off the elevator and ran to the parking lot. She jumped into the car and locked the doors. Just as she was pulling off Streets grabbed ahold of the door handle. Monica threw the car and drive. Streets banged on the windows and bust open the driver's window with his fist. He was doing everything in his power to get ahold of her. It was more so the camera he wanted than the money. If what happened gotten out, his life was destroyed. He grabbed Monica by her hair and began to pull it.

"Ahhhh!" Monica screamed as she felt her hair ripping out of her head. That didn't stop her though. She pressed down on the gas. RMMM! The car made a loud noise. She literally drug Streets' naked body out of the parking lot.

His body rubbed up against the concrete causing his flesh to tear open. He tried to let go of the car but was stuck. "AHHHHHHHH!" He screamed in agony. The pain was unbearable. His right arm was snatched out the socket.

Monica swerved and hit a car and Streets' body rolled all over the ground. Half of the skin was missing from his body, his right arm was inches away from the socket, and his face was bruised and scareed up. Monica continued to drive off in the dusk. She glanced back at Streets who was lying on the ground fighting for his life. She didn't give a damn. She was minutes away from her destination. She was going to dump the car, pick up her 2 kids and take a bus down to South Carolina. She was now paid out the ass and could give her kids the life they deserved. Streets nor Leo would ever hear from her or see her black ass again.

Leo stood back and disbelief. He couldn't believe what went down in front of his very own eyes. Instead of sticking around for any police involvement, he eased back to the room. He then got dressed, got his belongings and got the hell out of dodge. He was pissed off that he didn't have any money. He felt so hopeless and broke that he could kill a motherfucker. On his cab ride to Michelle's house he came up with a quick idea. He was just about to rob the cab driver until the cab driver got pulled over. Leo sat in the back shitting bricks. He decided to get dropped off at Michelle's house without taking anything from anyone.

CHAPTER 9

Michelle was pissed the fuck off. She got up and managed to get dressed in a pair of sweat pants and a t-shirt. She grabbed her car keys off the nightstand and left out the house. She looked at her gas meter and noticed that it was on empty. She didn't give any fucks about her gas or that annoying ass alerting sound it kept making. She went straight to the liquor store where she purchased herself a 5th of Paul Masson and a pack of cigarettes— which she didn't smoke, but with all the chaos that was going on in her life it was literally driving her insane and driving her outside of her normal routine. She couldn't even think straight anymore. Her life was so fucked up that all she wanted back was her man, take the blow job back that she gave Luke, the pussy back she gave Leo and live a happy life with her man and their unborn child. Walking back to the car, she drug her feet as she moved at a slow pace.

"Damn, she look like shit." She heard a female say.

Michelle turned around just in time to see a young group of females staring at her. Ignoring them she kept heading towards her car.

"What the fuck that hoe looking at?" Another one of the young females asked.

Michelle shook her head. She went to her car and placed her bag inside of it. Then she popped her trunk and before she knew it she was outside of the liquor store swinging a steel baseball bat.

WHAM! WHAM! WHAM! Michelle swung the bat, hitting the young girls. Her eyes were closed and she completely lost all control. One of the girls snatched the bat from Michelle. WHAM! She knocked Michelle upside of her head so damn hard that she almost passed out. She stumbled backwards into her car, losing her balance. Three of the females came running towards her. Michelle fell onto the ground and sheltered her face with her hands. She had yet again wrote a check that her ass couldn't cash.

"Bitch you got the right ones today!" One of the girls screamed.

Kicks, punches and hits covered Michelle's aching body from the top of her head down to her ankles.

She balled herself up in a fetal position as these girls beat the brakes off her ass. At that moment she gave up and wished that they had killed her because the way she was feeling she didn't give a damn or any fucks anymore. She was still lying on the ground, sobbing her heart out and the girls had left minutes ago. Her heart, body, soul and mind was so numb that she didn't realize that the brutal beating that she had received was over.

Michelle came out of hiding, not seeing the girls in sight. She got up and hauled ass to her car and pulled off. She pulled over to the nearest gas station to get gas.

"What the fuck do you mean my card has been declined!" Michelle yelled at the store clerk. She was on a rampage. She was ready to snatch his Arabic ass up from behind the counter and put a hurting on his ass. "No bitch, that's your momma's card you are reading! Now slide my shit again!" She said for sure that she had money in the bank.

He slid it again and handed Michelle her card back/ "You have no money in the bank." He said wearing a cute smile.

Michelle snatched her card up. Storming back to her car she used her car phone and dialed mobile banking.

"Your balance is negative -$8,755.02," the pleasant operator said over the phone.

Michelle couldn't believe her ears. She hung up the phone and dialed the number again as if she wasn't hearing the correct shit. Once again she heard the same exact thing. She thought about her attackers and them taking her purse.

Michelle shook her head, which was spinning so much that she thought she was going to pass out. She was in pure disbelief. She had been robbed for everything that was to her name. Michelle snatched the bottle up from the passenger seat and took the entire thing down in a few gulps. Starting her car she drove back to her place.

Confined behind her closed doors she began to spaz out. "AHHHH!" She screamed out of control. Going on an angry rampage she began knocking things over and snatching pictures off the walls. She was in a petty and bitchy mood. She ran into the kitchen, snatching the refrigerator door open she started throwing its contents all over the floors.

"FUCK MY LIFE! WHY ME? WHY ME?" She screamed at top of her lungs.

When she was done tearing up the downstairs of her home, it looked like a hurricane hand run through.

Michelle huffed and threw herself down on the edge of the sofa that she had knocked over. "What the fuck am I going to do? Why me?" She questioned herself. She rubbed her hand across her stomach and thoughts of her unborn appeared.

She wasn't thinking rationally at all. She jogged up the stairs, rushing to the bathroom and threw things out of the cabinets. Her eyes lit up when she came across a set of clippers. She plugged the clippers in and before she knew it she had completely shaved off the right side of her head.

"Ahhh what the fuck?" She cried when she looked in the mirror and realized what the hell she had just done.

With a corrupt expression painted on her face she stared at the reflection. She was a complete mess with snot running out of her nose, her lips were dry and crusty, her face was all bruised and banged up, her eye were buried and were close to being black. She felt like hell and appeared as if she had been through hell and back. She sat down on the toilet and cried her eyes out. The slumber that she was slowly entering into would sure enough be the death of her if she didn't get herself together.

Hearing a loud knock at her door, she jumped to her feet. Swinging the door open she was ready to air the visitor out until she saw Leo standing there wearing a smile on his face.

"Was that you in here screaming baby?" he questioned.

Michelle threw herself into his arms. She couldn't refrain from crying her little heart out.

Leo's shirt was lathered in tears in a matter of seconds. He patted Michelle's back softly and rubbed his hands through her hair, standing in the doorframe of her house.

Their eyes locked for a split second. Leo grabbed her by her chin gently and slid his tongue deep into her warm mouth. Not breaking lose from the immaculate tongue locking, Michelle backed further into the house. Leo closed the door with his right foot.

He quickly glanced around at the house at the mess. "What happened?" He asked.

Michelle shrugged. "Anger issues."

He laughed at her. "Anger issues huh?" He picked her up and she wrapped her legs around his waist. "What's the matter?" He asked her. "Who laid their hands on you? Who do I have to kill now?"

Michelle smiled at the fact that Leo was concerned about her wellbeing and wanted to know who was in her life causing chaos. She sighed. "Well today has been horrible. First that shit happened with JaKai, then some girls at the liquor jumped me for no apparent reason at all. Hating ass bitches!" She huffed. "Then not to mention I was robbed earlier today. Someone wiped me clean from everything I had." She began to break down and cry again when she thought about the terrible loss she had taken.

He shook his head. "Damn baby, you been through hell. So I have I. But don't worry about a thing. We are going to get back right together. You and I." He assured her.

Michelle stared into his eyes. Unless he was God and could make miracles happen in 2.3 seconds she wasn't trying to hear a damn thing he was saying. "How is that going to happen?" She raised her eyebrow.

"Steal, rob and kill. However we can get ourselves back." Leo smiled.

Michelle shook her head.

"Don't you work at a bank?" He questioned.

She nodded. "Kind of sort of. I don't know if I still have my job or not." She said thinking about how she was going to go back to her job the following Monday and try to rekindle things with her lovely boss.

"Let's go tomorrow and try and get a loan. You get like ten stacks and I can flip that shit and have us back to where we need to be. You can leave that no good nigga and come live with me. I'll treat you like the queen that you deserve to be treated like." He winked as he lied through his teeth.

Michelle thought for a second. "We will see in the morning."

Leo nodded. *'We will see after I lay this good dick on you,'* he thought. He carried Michelle up the steps, stripped her and kissed every inch of her aching body.

Michelle's chest heaved as Leo blessed her entire body. Climbing up to her chest, their lips locked. Michelle took his tongue inside her mouth and their tongues danced. Michelle could literally smell the dick on his breath but took it as him just having bad breath period. She didn't know she was kissing the man that was just sucking her 1st cousins dick earlier that night.

Leo eased down her stomach and met her throbbing kitty. He pushed her legs to the side and dove deep inside her.

"Ohhhh Leo! Yessss!" Michelle cried.

Leo licked the hell out of her pussy, giving her the award winning prize to get what he wanted and needed from her. No matter what he had to do, she was going to carry her ass on to the bank in the morning and get that loan for him. Lifting his head up, which was covered in sweet juices, he flipped Michelle over on her back. He pulled her back so her ass could be in the air.

"Ohhhh! Shitttt!" Michelle legs shook when Leo entered her from behind. Her pussy wrapped around his dick like the perfect match.

Leo stroked her insides, hard and long as if with each stroke there was purpose behind it. He kissed her on the nape of her neck and fucked her.

She laid in his arms and thought about getting that loan for him, packing her shit and being with him. He was fine as hell, the dick was flamboyant, and the sweet nothings he was feeding into her brain had her damn near lost in a daze of his.

Just like Leo knew Michelle would do, he woke up in the morning to her cleaning the entire house. While she was cleaning he crawled out of the bed, making his way to her kitchen and stood there butter ball naked. Then he slaved over her stove, making them a full course breakfast.

Michelle was impressed when Leo came walking out the kitchen with two plates for them in his hands. After she scarfed her breakfast down, she carried her ass to that bank and was approved for a $20,000 loan, which she told Leo that she was only approved for $5,000. Like the dummy he and many other men made her out to be, she had handed the $5,000 over to Leo who promised her he would be back with $10,000 to put in her pockets.

Once Leo left, Michelle got dressed, covered all her bruises in her MAC makeup and went to the hospital to check on Cookie. It had been a few days since she had been missing in action and she felt terrible for not being by Cookie's bedside.

"Hey boo. I'm back," she said, pulling up at chair closer to the bed. "I been through hell and back and I'm surprised I'm still standing baby. I don't know if it was the man upstairs who is carrying me today or that good ole dick that I was served last night that put a little inspiration and motivation back into my life." Hearing her own humor she burst into laughter. She was laughing so damn hard that she was in tears. For the first time in a long time they were good tears. Smelling the stench of the old hospital, Michelle pulled out her Love Spell and sprayed it into the air. "Much better." She said aloud. Michelle pulled out her makeup and began getting Cookie made up while she told her everything that had went down in the past few days. It felt so damn good that she was able to finally let someone in on her life, besides Leo, who she didn't know if he was full of shit or not. Regardless that didn't matter. He served a purpose in her life at that moment and that was taming her hormones, keeping her company and that was about it. Sure she wanted to be loved, but if it didn't happen there she was sure to find it somewhere else. By the time Michelle got done telling her life story of disaster, heartbreak and pain she was in tears, reliving each moment.

Cookie could hear everything Michelle was saying and was heartbroken by her being heartbroken. She began moving her fingers, letting Michelle know her words weren't going unheard and her pain was no longer just her pain, that it was hers too.

Michelle's eyes lit up when she noticed Cookie's hands moving. She covered her mouth in amazement. "NURSE! NURSE!" She screamed. She ran out into the hallway and was in complete shock when she saw JaKai wheeling himself down the hall…

CHAPTER 10

JaKai decided to do something out the ordinary for Nia. He knew that she was enduring a great amount of pain. Some in which he contributed to, so he wanted to make her feel special because truthfully she was special in his eyes. And now that she was carrying his first child, she was even more special. So with that being said, he called Luke up and had Luke go purchase a nice gown for Nia. He then called up his personal check which he only used on special events him and Luke threw together for the city. He then went online and ordered Nia twenty dozen long stem red roses which were placed in 5-pound heart shaped vases. He then ordered her a 5-foot teddy bear. When he got the call that his order was filled and was on its way, he got himself dressed in the black slacks and Gucci button up that Luke had brought him to the hospital. Luke and Taylor, Alesha, Luke's mother, and Nikki all stood out in the hallway while Nia was peacefully sleeping. They all were in awe about JaKai's surprise. JaKai out did himself for the first time. He was a hood nigga but also had a heart of gold for the right one who was able to make him share it when he felt like it was hidden deep down inside of him.

Luke's heart glowed when the deliverers made their way towards Nia's room.

******

Nia had gotten up from her bed and slid into her slippers. She was in a lot of pain but JaKai was on her mind. She had sent him a text but didn't get a reply back. So she decided to find him. She opened the door to her room and was in for a surprise.

Michelle was storming towards JaKai, when she spotted Luke and everyone standing outside of the room. She was ready to give them the show of their life. She was pissed that she had left her purse back in Cookie's room. Inside of her purse she had a pocket knife which would have done some damage at the moment. When she saw the delivery people walking up to JaKai holding oversized heart shape vases with long stem roses in them she damn near died. Her pride was damaged and her heart was broken. She saw Nia peek her head out the door, and even at her worse Nia still looked breath taking. Michelle covered her mouth so that no one could hear the loud scream of hurt that was trying to escape. She turned around and ran out the hospital. She didn't even get a chance to see Cookie waking up for the first time in weeks, and sadly Michelle was the first person who Cookie asked about...

CHAPTER 11

Nia stepped outside of her room. "JAKAI!" She whined, covering her mouth. The deliverers walked past her and began placing all the roses in her room. "What am I going to do with all these roses! Boy you are something else!" She grabbed her chest and was cheesing.

JaKai pulled Nia down on his lap. "Do what you want with them. I wanted to show you how much I love you." He said. He grabbed the oversized teddy bear and placed it in her lap.

Nia took both of her arms and wrapped them around it, and mushed her face in tit to kiss it. She felt like a big kid on her birthday.

JaKai grabbed her by her chin and they embraced into a deep kiss. "I promise you, we are going to be good." He told her.

Everyone was aweing and all googly-eyed from all the love and romance.

Nia got up and went and grabbed a vase of roses. She handed Taylor a vase, her mother, Alesha and Luke's mother a vase.

Luke shook his head. Now he was going to have to do something to top JaKai's romance for Taylor. He had to make his girl feel special as well.

Nikki was happy that her daughter finally had a good dude in her life, instead of all the no good ones that she entertained. Being that her daughter was already pregnant there was nothing much she could do but accept her happiness. Seeing the two of them all lovely dovey she thought about the nigga she had been entertaining the past couple of weeks who usually was calling her back to back. Which was odd that he didn't contact her in the past 2 days.

JaKai watched Nia while she handed the vases out. She was the perfect match for him. He made a promise that he was going to do right by her.

Nia sat on JaKai's lap. He had outdone himself Nia had thought. But yet she didn't see half the life that JaKai had to offer her. There was way more than what she had gotten so far.

Everyone went to Nia's room and they all sat around and talked for a few. Once everyone started to separate, Nia was more than happy to see their loved ones go.

JaKai was resting in her bed, so she got up and closed the door behind her. Her kitty was purring but being that it was still aching and she was still bleeding she couldn't do anything about it. That didn't stop her from crawling between JaKai's legs and giving him the blow job of a lifetime. She sucked him so damn good he fell asleep in her arms.

CHAPTER 12

Cookie was sad as hell not seeing Michelle there when she awoke. She was fighting for weeks and she was sure she was going to pull through everything. There was no way she could give up so easily. After asking for Michelle who was nowhere to be found, JaKai crossed her mind. JaKai had totally disrespected her and if it was the last thing she did, she was going to get the last laugh. JaKai had something coming for him and it was going to be way sooner than later.

The doctors urgently took care of Cookie, running all types of tests on her to make sure she was functioning properly. All she kept asking about was her sister Michelle. Just as she was sitting up, her parents came walking in the room. Her eyes lit up. She blinked a few times to hold the tears back. She hadn't seen her parents in so long.

"Hey." She softly spoke.

Her mother rushed to her side and embraced her daughter. Whether Cookie knew it or not they were by her side. Fighting and praying for her.

Her father wanted to hate her so much. He wanted his son Michael back. The son who he showed tough love to. The son who he pushed so hard so that he could be the best man he could be. Instead, all of that pushing and tough love turned his son into something he never thought his son would be. It was a disaster at first and for a long time. But truth to be told, deep down inside he loved his child. Although he didn't let it show as much, especially since Michelle had come to his house and raised hell. After the first visit seeing Cookie lying there fighting for her life, he had a change of heart.

"I'm sorry," her father began.

Cookie shook her head. "Please don't apologize to me. We are all humans and we make mistakes. I just want you all to accept me for who I am. Because at the end of the day, I'm a child of God just like everyone else."

Both Cookie's parents nodded. Cookie was absolutely right. A parent should love their child no matter what. From that day and forward her father was going to be the best father he could be to his children. He had made amends with Cookie and wanted to have a heart to heart with Michelle to see what was going on with her as well. Just as her parents got comfortable, two police officers knocked at the door.

Seeing them a devious smile came across Cookie's face. PAYBACK WAS A BITCH!

******

Streets laid up in the hospital bed fighting for his life. He had three surgeries and was still hanging on. All of his family had been contacted, and the doctors were expecting him to turn for the worst. Hours later his family gathered in the room and prayed. Michelle's mother was overwhelmed. First Michael, now Streets was laid up in the hospital fighting for his life…

CHAPTER 13

Taylor finally made her way home. Luke parked down the street from her house, killed the ignition and glanced over at Taylor. Her bedroom eyes were lit up as she stared out the window.

"What you thinking about?" Luke asked her.

Taylor sighed. "So much has happened today. I just want to go take a hot shower and get some rest. I'm ready to start living life. Today Nia showed me that life was too short. I'm no longer going to allow anyone or anything to hold me back. I know I'm young but I also know exactly what I want."

Luke nodded. "Do you want to go get a bite to eat before you head in?" He asked her.

Taylor smiled for a second. Hell she was already late being home so why not enjoy herself before her parents got ahold of her.

"Why the heck not? I know my ass is already grass." Taylor laughed to herself.

Luke started the car up and Taylor sat back in her seat. Luke drove around the city and ended up going to a seafood restaurant in Greenbelt, Maryland, which was located off the docks.

The two of them ordered a shit load of seafood and Luke ordered a bottle of wine for himself. Taylor was pregnant and he wasn't having her drinking and possibly harming his child.

He cracked the hard shell on Taylor's snow crab for her and peeled all the meat out like she was some sort of baby. Taylor loved the way he treated her, like she deserved to be treated.

She leaned over the table and Luke fed her the crab meat dipped in butter. Taylor took the crab meat and started to giggle. She looked up at Luke.

Luke shook his head. She was so innocent in his eyes. He hoped that he had gotten himself into the right thing. Age played a main factor between the two of them. He was hoping he wasn't rushing Taylor into growing up way too fast. But at the end of the day he hoped that she was able to fulfill his needs and the main thing he needed was a woman. A real woman at that.

After they got done eating they ate desert. Luke was on his way to take Taylor back home, but his dick had other plans. So instead he stopped by his condo.

"I have to run in here for a few and take care of something." He told Taylor.

Taylor knew what line of business Luke was in, so she nodded.

He stepped out the car and went to the passenger side and opened Taylor's door. He then went to the trunk to pull out 2 duffle bags.

Once inside of his condo, he went to his safe and began putting the contents inside of it. Taylor watched as he piled stacks of cash and bricks of cocaine into the safes. It was evident that Luke was getting it and she was impressed. With him, she had no financial worries. Luke was the man and she for sure was going to be set for the rest of her life.

When he got done, he took Taylor out to his patio that oversaw the entire downtown area of Washington. Taylor looked off into the night life. Luke walked up behind her and wrapped his arms around her small waist. Softly he placed kisses all over the back of her neck. At his touch, Taylor's little hairs on her neck rose. He ran his hands all over her flat stomach then slowly he crept his way up to her breast. Pulling her erected breast out of her top, he softly pinched her nipples and began to play with him between his middle and index finger.

"Mmmm." Taylor moaned throwing her head back.

Luke slid his hand in her pants and it roamed its way down to her fresh kitty. He eased his fingers into her highly drenched opening, and moved his fingers in and out of her at a fast pace.

"Ohhhh." She moaned. She lifted her leg and propped it up on the banister. Luke was definitely grooming a young freak.

"Take all of this shit off." He told her.

Taylor looked around. Luke pulling at her clothing gave her the motivation she needed to strip. They were on the 37th floor up in the air. If anyone saw them, neither gave a damn.

Luke got on his knees, lifting Taylor's leg above his head. e feasted at her goodies like it was a delicious Thanksgiving dinner. Lifting Taylor up in the air, her legs were wrapped around his neck. He turned her around and propped her on the banister.

Taylor was in her own world. She lifted her head and opened her eyes. Seeing that she was hanging over half of the city of Washington, noticing the people looked like little ants below, she began to panic. "Luke! What are you doing! Let me down." Being freaked out her legs starting to shake with fear. One bad move and she was a goner for sure.

Luke grabbed her by her ankles tightly. "Do you trust me?" He asked rising to his feet. Holding her tightly he stared her deep into her eyes. "Do you trust me." He softly pecked her on the lips, not breaking the eye battle the two was sharing.

Taylor's chest heaved.

"Relax and enjoy." He told her. Luke was more than spontaneous. Taylor didn't know whether she should be scared or what. Nonetheless everything was about Luke. She trusted him.

He got back down, holding her with all his will. He feasted on her pussy. She was nothing but ooh's and ah's as he damn near licked her into a coma. She held onto the banister, holding all 175 pounds of her weight up with everything in her.

She softly threw her head back. "AHHHH GAWDDD LUKE!" She screamed so damn loud that half the city could have possibly heard her sexual cries.

Luke helped her down, pulling his pants down. His hard dick broke out of his pants and boxers like an escaped prisoner.

Taylor bent over with her ass tooted in the air. Seeing the beautiful city view and Taylor's fat scrumptious ass, Luke was in heaven. He rammed his dick inside of Taylor, fucking her to oblivion.

Afterwards the two showered together. Luke hated the fact he had to take Taylor back home. He pleaded and begged her to just stay with him but she told him after she finished school she was all his, so he did as she asked him to do and took her home.

They pulled up a few houses from Taylor's.

Luke planted light kisses all over Taylor's face. Their lips locked into an unlimited kiss that seem like it was going to last an eternity until Taylor broke away.

"I love you Luke." She told him stepping out the car.

Luke smiled and started his ignition. "I'll see you tomorrow shorty." He told her.

Once Taylor disappeared behind the single family homes he pulled off into the night.

CHAPTER 14

The night for Luke was still young. He wasn't ready to retire to his home. So instead he went to a little after hour strip joint. Stepping inside he regretted that he even wasted his time. Every bitch in the club looked like they were shot up with bullet holes, track marks, odd looking bodies and bad weaves. The place was named 'Tasty Night Club' but there sure as hell wasn't nothing in there tasty whatsoever. It should have been named disaster because every female in the club looked as if she had been through something.

Sitting at the bar, Luke ordered a double shot of Henny and Coke. Sad to say, the bartender was the most appealing thing in there. Her short hair was styled in an ear length bob and little gold stud earrings were in her ears. Her makeup was done to perfection. She had a black collar like choker around her neck, with a matching black half top and skirt. Her caramel skin was flawless. "What brings you here baby?" She flirted with Luke.

Luke looked at her and smiled. "The night is still young," was all he was able to come up with, rather than telling her that boredom had brought him there. He could have went to one of his traps, bagged up some coke and did some other work. But he chose not to, because he really didn't move to much without his right hand man who was laid up in the hospital.

After a few drinks Luke was on. He stared at the bartender. Standing up he could barely make it to his car. He slid two hundred dollar bills on the bar. "What time you get off?" He asked the bartender who now was looking sexy as fuck in his drunken eyes.

"In fifteen more minutes." She flirted, running her tongue across her paper thin lips.

Luke nodded and lifted his wrist looking at his Rolex. His vision was so damn blurred he could barely see the time. "Let me get two bottles of water." He told her.

Walking off she went to retrieve the two bottles of water. Bending over with her head in the refrigerator, Luke scoped out her ass. His dick instantly became brick. It was about to be ON!

She came back handed him the bottles of water and purposely grabbed ahold of his soft hands. She licked her lips. "Do you want me to meet you at your car?" She asked him.

Luke nodded and turned to walk away. Sitting in his car waiting those fifth teen minutes, he debated if he should pull off or not. When the bartender came strutting to his car, his thoughts were put on hold.

"This you?" She smiled swinging the passenger door open.

Luke started the car but didn't put it in drive. Looking at her, his vision was slowly coming back to life and she wasn't what he thought he saw inside of the bar. Maybe it was the alcohol or the lights. Whatever the hell it was, it wasn't doing nothing for him.

She could tell by the look on Luke's face that something was wrong. She quickly lightened the mood. She crawled over in the driver's seat and sat on his lap. "What's really up with you?" She licked her lips.

Luke stared into her eyes but didn't say anything.

He reclined the seat back and she slowly unbuckled his pants. Luke didn't stop her from lowering herself between his legs or from pulling out his Mandingo. Highly impressed with the size of his manhood she wrapped her lips around it.

Luke laid his head back. A few moans escaped his mouth as she slowly and seductively made love to his dick.

******

Taylor lied in her bed. Luke was all over her mind. The way he took control of her body and the way he made her so damn submissive. He was daddy for sure in her eyes. She wanted him to love her and wanted to do nothing more than love him and make him happy.

Thinking about him, she became moist between her thighs. In the dark she slid her hands inside of her loose fitting pajamas. Vivid images of Luke's long and thick pole played in her mind. The way it felt so damn good inside of her made her stroke her insides like no other. She pinched her nipples and slid her finger into her opening.

"Lukeeee." She softly whispered while pleasuring herself.

Her fingers were soaking wet. She wished Luke was there to fuck her the way she needed to be fucked. Him taking control of her body and taking her to a higher measure of pure pleasure.

Spreading her legs a bit wider she eased a second finger inside of her opening. "Oohhh." She sexually cried, while discovering her best hot spot. Thoughts of sneaking out the house and calling Luke crossed her mind. The way she was feeling she needed some dick so damn bad that it didn't matter that she just got broken off properly by him. The way his head game was set up, she couldn't get enough of it.

She turned over on her back and pushed her knees to her chest. "Ohhh." She moaned in the enjoyable moment. Her eyes squeezed tightly shut and she bit down on her bottom lip.

She didn't once hear her bedroom door open, nor see the rays of light that entered her bedroom.

Her father eased into the room, witnessing his beloved daughter pleasure herself and call out a grown man's name in pleasure. He was pretty heated. He had noticed that Taylor had just walked in the house through the backdoor moments prior, which he almost got caught because he was sneaking and creeping as well.

He slid the leather belt out of the loops on his slacks. The belt hung from his side. Walking over to the bed, he peered down at Taylor. Shaking his head, he snatched the blankets off of her, exposing her.

Taylor's eyes flung open. "DADDY!" She cried.

Her father lifted the belt and went ham on Taylor's ass. WHAM! WHAM! WHAM! The belt connected against her body.

"WHAT THE HELL YOU THINK YOU ARE IN MY HOUSE DOING? NOT UNDER MY ROOF! THEN YOUR FAST ASS JUST CAME IN HERE AT 3 IN THE MORNING!" He yelled.

Taylor's mother was lying bed. She woke up to all the commotion. She jumped to her feet, and with her breast slinging and hanging she flew into Taylor's room.

Taylor tried to stand to her feet but her father knocked her right back down on her ass.

"STOP IT! STOP IT! I'M PREGNANT!" Taylor screamed in fear that her father was going to kill her and her unborn child.

"Pregnant?" Her mother softly repeated.

"PREGNANT! YOUR ASS IS GOOD AS DEAD!" Her father yelled. He lost all control. Taylor had just shattered his heart into a million pieces. Not his baby girl. He couldn't dare sit back and allow her to fuck up her life with a worthless no good ass nigga. He threw the belt to the side, before he knew it. He was beating Taylor with his fist like he was in a street fight with a nigga who just disrespected him, or even worse just stole from him. Which Taylor did none of the two.

Taylor fell onto the floor. She balled up in a fetal position, doing everything in her will to protect her unborn child.

The powerful punches her father was sending to her was putting her body in a tremendous amount of pain. Her mother realized the brutal attack was way too much for her liking, so she stepped forward to protect her daughter.

"Steven! Have you lost your damn mind." She squealed grabbing ahold of his arm.

His arm flew back and elbowed her in her eye. Losing balance, she fell back and hit her body against the dresser. She quickly stood to her feet, ignoring the pain she was in and charged at angry husband. "GET BACK WOMAN!" He screamed knocking her in the same eye again with his elbow.

"AHHH!" She cried.

Taylor jumped up on her feet and began vomiting. Trying to make it to the door, her father was still on her ass. He snatched up by her hair and rammed her face into the wall. Taylor for sure thought she was going to wind out on the opposite side of the wall. But she didn't. Sliding her foot back, she kicked him in the balls.

He grabbed ahold of his balls and stumbled back a bit. Taylor ran out the door and was rushing down the steps. Her father ran in the hallway, seeing the small lamp resting on the stand. He picked it up and WHAM! He knocked Taylor in the back of her head.

Taylor felt like she was going to pass out. She couldn't stay a second in her father's house.

She fumbled with the front door trying to get it unlocked, and seeing her father on her tail she hauled ass into the kitchen. She snatched up a butcher's knife out of the holder and backed up against the back door. "IF YOU DARE COME NEAR ME I WILL FUCKING KILL YOU!" She said through gritted teeth. She had enough of her father and she saw that it was either kill or be killed between the two of them. She didn't know about her father but she had a purpose to serve and he wasn't going to be the death of her.

"I MADE YOU AND I SURE AS HELL WILL TAKE YOU RIGHT OFF THIS EARTH!" He yelled.

Taylor stared coldly into her father's eyes and noticed that something was off with him. She instantly assumed that he was on some sort of drugs or something. He was too damn angry and had too damn much energy for his own good.

"I HATE YOU! I DON'T EVER WANT TO SEE YOU AGAIN!" She yelled.

Her father laughed and came charging towards her. Unexpectedly Taylor raised the knife and began slicing and dicing at her father.

Taylor's mother rushed into the kitchen just in time to see Taylor cutting her father up like chop suey.

"AHHH YOU LITTLE BITCH!" He screamed out in agony.

Taylor was beyond hurt.

Steven stood back and observed the damage that his daughter had done to his arm. Four stab wounds didn't give him any fear.

"STEVEN! WHAT THE HELL HAS GOTTEN INTO YOU!"

Taylor fumbled with the doorknob, keeping her knife raised and her eyes on her father.

He came charging at her yet again. This time Taylor sent a deep stab to his chest.

"AHHHH SHIT!" He roared.

The knife was still stuck in his flesh, and Taylor took that opportunity to get the hell out of his site. She ran all the way to the gas station. Using the phone inside she called Luke.

****

"FUCK! FUCK!" Luke screamed. Grabbing the back of the girl's head he shot his hot cum down her throat.

She caught and swallowed every drop of it like the hoe she was. She was so damn nasty that Luke was turned the hell off.

His cellphone started ringing and without looking at the caller ID he answered it.

"LUKE!" Taylor cried.

Hearing Taylor's devastated voice, Luke sat up in his seat. He could hear her crying. "Where are you?" was the only questioned he wanted to know.

Taylor told him where she was and Luke looked over at the female who was sliding her pants off. Reaching over her, he opened the passenger door. He couldn't believe that she didn't get the fucking hint and it was time to dismiss herself. Luke threw her ass out of his car along with her belongings and drove like a bat out of hell to pick Taylor up.

He pulled up to the gas station in less than twenty minutes. Seeing Taylor standing there with blood all over her clothing and shaking, his heart dropped. His blood pressure jumped sky high and his blood was boiling. Somebody was going to die. One thing he didn't play with was his loved ones. Then when it came to his unborn child, that took him to a place where there was no coming back.

He jumped out of his car, rushing to Taylor, and she fell right into his arms.

In a matter of seconds, his shirt was drenched with tears. Pulling himself back he looked into her eyes. He softly grabbed her cherubic face, trying not to touch the bruises that were there. "Where is he?" He asked.

Taylor cried. "It was my father." She cried.

Luke shook his head in disbelief. He helped Taylor into the passenger seat of the car and reclined the seat back as far as it could so that she could sit without any complications.

He pulled up to Taylor's father house like a mad man.

Reaching across Taylor he unlocked his glove compartment and pulled out a steel 9mm.

Taylor shook her. "Luke please don't kill him." She begged him, tugging at his shirt.

Luke was so mad that the veins in his forehead were pulsating and his hands was shaking.

"He's my father." Taylor cried, grabbing Luke by his arm again.

Luke gazed at her. "You should have thought about that before you called me." He told her, snatching his arm away. He kicked open his driver door.

Getting out of the car, the strong demeanor he held could read all hell was about to be caused. Approaching her front door, he didn't bother knocking. He kicked that damn door in and it loosely fell off the hinges. All the lights were on in the house. Luke jogged up the steps taking them 3 by 3.

Taylor's father had just jumped up when hearing the door being kicked it. He suspected that his daughter probably would have called the police on him after what he had done which he was the least sorry about.

Coming out the bedroom and seeing Luke coming to his daughter's rescue he was furious. He cursed himself for leaving his shot gun in the closet.

The two grown men stared at each other. Both with hatred embedded in their eyes. Luke because of what he had done to his lover, his child's mother. Taylor father's because he hated that Luke's grown ass was trying to take his daughter from him and turn her into a grown woman too quickly.

"You came in the right household today." Taylor's father laughed.

He cracked his knuckles.

"Honey gon head and call the paramedics and tell them we had an intruder and he's now dead." He called out to his wife.

Luke wasn't hearing shit he had to say. He wanted to kill her father at the first sight of him. But first he wanted to make sure he felt that shit. He wanted to beat him senseless until he was begging for God to have mercy on his soul. Luke went charging him, sweeping him off his feet.

The two tussled around in the long hallway.

Steven, being a wrestler in high school and some in college, used his old skills finally. He flipped Luke over on his back. Luke had him by at least 60 pounds but that didn't mean shit to him. He grabbed Luke's right arm and forced it behind his neck. He then wrapped his arms around Luke's neck, trying to choke the life out of him.

Luke's eyes rolled to the back of his head. With all the strength in him Luke stood to his feet. Grabbing Steven's arm he flipped him over on his back. Hovering over him, Luke sent punches to his face, back to back, blackening both of his eyes with only a few hits each. He then began stomping the life out of Taylor's father. Luke kept going until his chest slowly heaved.

Taylor's mother came rushing into the hallway holding a shotgun. "ENOUGH!" She roared, gripping the trigger tightly.

Luke stopped. Looking up at her he smiled. He saw where Taylor inherited her natural beauty. Seeing her mother standing angelically in her night gown he also saw where all of Taylor's crazy curves came from. Luke threw his hands up in the air. "You know what he did was wrong." He spat.

Her mother didn't blink. Instead she aimed the shot gun towards Luke's manhood. "And what you did to MY daughter was wrong!" She spat back.

Luke shook his head. "I love your daughter…It was nice meeting the two of you." He said. He then turned around and left out the house.

Going back to the car, Taylor was looking out the window with wide eyes. Seeing Luke's shirt stained in blood she expected the worst.

Taylor didn't have to question Luke whether it be love or not. She knew for sure that he loved her like no other and most importantly he was so loyal to her that he would do whatever it took to protect her to protect their unborn child.

Luke got into the car and pulled off full speed.

Leaving her parents' house that night Taylor made the ultimate decision. Her parents or Luke. Of course she chose her lover Luke.

Instead of going to his condo, he took Taylor all the way out to his house, which was now going to be *their* house.

CHAPTER 15

A month later…

Alesha had finally got ahold of Streets. She had found out he was in the hospital. Skipping school, she took a cab to the hospital. After getting his room number, she stood in front of his room door. She exhaled and sighed, debating whether or not should she stay or turn around and go.

Deciding to stay, she extended her hand and knocked on the door.

"Who the fuck is it?" Street screamed from the other side of the door.

Alesha shook her head. "It's me Alesha." She said in a soft voice but loud enough for Streets to hear her.

At the hearing of her voice Streets' heart began to flutter. Out of all the bitches he done fucked and trust he had a lot of bitches, Alesha the youngest of them all, was the only one to be able to make him feel like he wanted to love and be loved.

"Come in." He changed his tone.

Walking inside the room, Streets stared at Alesha. He couldn't help but to do so. She was so damn gorgeous and innocent looking that it turned him on.

"How are you?" Alesha said walking towards the window.

Streets gazed at her plump rear end for a split second.

"I'm alive." He replied.

Alesha turned around. "That's a blessing." She pleasantly smiled.

Although Streets hated life at that moment, Alesha's warmness made him smile for the first time in months.

Alesha walked towards him and touched the side of face, which was all bandaged up.

Streets damn near melted at her touch. Alesha leaned forward and kissed Streets' dry lips softly.

Streets was a bit taken back by her forwardness but he didn't say nothing about it. He actually liked that she was now stepping up. Hell had he known all it took was for him to be laid up in the hospital for Alesha to bring her ass around then he would have been faked an accident or some shit.

"So tell me, what happened?" Streets said wanting to know everything that happened between Alesha and him.

Alesha sighed then grabbed a chair and sat down beside him while playing with her nails.

"Well after the first time we messed around, I started feeling weird. I liked you a lot but I think it was too much for the both of our own good. Not to mention my family doesn't allow me to date. Then I found out I was pregnant. I didn't know what to do. All I thought about was getting rid of the child before you or anyone else found out." She softly spoke.

Streets stared at her waiting for her to continue but she didn't. He cleared his throat.

"Did you once think about me? Did you think I had a say so in what you did with my seed?" He asked.

Alesha sighed, throwing her one leg across the other. "I wasn't thinking. That's the problem." She said.

Streets shook his head. He wasn't so upset that Alesha got rid of their child. He was more upset that she came into his life, drove him crazy then straight dipped on his ass.

The two of them grew quiet for a few minutes.

"I'm sorry Johnathan." Alesha said breaking the silence.

"Come here." Streets told her.

Alesha got up and slowly climbed onto the bed next to him.

"You don't ever have to be sorry with me." He said pecking her on her forehead.

Alesha was started to feel all warm inside. The way Streets made her feel was like the first time he ever kissed her.

Streets softly kissed on her neck then squeezed his hands between her tight thighs. "You haven't been giving my goodies away, have you?"

Alesha shook her head.

"Get up and go lock the door." Streets told her.

Alesha got up and did as he told her. While she was locking the door, Streets took the opportunity to hit the button on his IV, pumping more morphine and other narcotics into his veins. He was in an incredible amount of pain, but no pain or anything was going to stop him from crawling up into Alesha.

He was sprung and had a habit worse than any crack addict.

Alesha walked back over to the bed.

Streets grabbed his phone and strolled through it. He found some Pretty Ricky to play.

"Strip for me Alesha. Show me how sorry you are. Show me how much you really miss me." He demanded.

"Baby grind on me
Relax your mind take your time on me
Let me get deeper shawty ride on me
Now come and sex me till yo body gets weak
Wit slow grindin baby
Grind on me
Relax your mind take your time on me
Let me get deeper shawty ride on me
Now come and sex me till yo body gets weak
Wit slow grindin baby
When I hit em I make'em say ahh
Sex be my day job
I hit em in the back of my car
Make em ride like a like a seesaw
I make'em laugh and giggle
Cuddle a little
Suck on the nipples lick the whip cream from the middle
Girlfirend I never go raw…"

Blared through the speakers of his phone. Alesha was a bit nervous at first but it wasn't like Johnathan hadn't seen her in her birthday suit before. She slowly moved her hips to the music and winded her body. Perfecting a special dance for Streets she turned around and touched her toes, removing her pants and her panties. She made her ass slowly jiggle. Reaching behind her, she softly slapped her ass, spreading her cheeks to the side. She gave Streets a peep at her shaven kitty from the back.

The devil, the doctors and whoever else said that Streets would never be able to get an erection again was a damn lie. At the sight of her perfectly, tight and pink kitty Streets' manhood grew damn near eight inches.

He couldn't take it anymore. He beckoned for Alesha. She seductively walked towards him, slowing placing one leg in front of the other with her hands on her hips. She licked her lips standing in front of him.

"Yes daddy." She softly cooed.

Streets damn near went wild. He was so damn horny and fully loaded that if his cum shot up out of him he was sure going to shoot a hole straight through the hospital's rooftop.

Alesha slowly climbed on top of Streets, slowly she worked her way all the way down his hardness. Her tight kitty gripped his dick tightly. Juices ran all down Streets' thigh. She stared him deep into his eyes.

"I love you girl!" Streets said to Alesha. Not saying it back, Alesha smiled. She slowly rode Streets' ass to town.

Before he could release his load inside of Alesha, she quickly jumped to her feet. She had skipped a few days of her birth control and she'd be damned if she got pregnant for a second time.

Streets leaned in and kissed her, holding her in his arms. He didn't ever want to let her go. The things that good pussy would do to a motherfucker.

CHAPTER 16

Michelle sat on the edge of her bed as Michael did her hair. She was so happy that her brother was alive and well. Despite a few minor scratches he was back to normal. She couldn't even imagine losing her brother who was her best friend. Michelle definitely needed Michael around. She was pregnant, lonely, miserable and vexed. She had every reason to be so. She was robbed three times. First with the men who broke into her house, second with Leo, who took off with her money and she hadn't heard from him since and thirdly by JaKai who stole her heart. He snatched it out of her chest and stomped all over it in front of her very eyes. She was now on some fuck niggas type of shit and was trying to get her money up by all means. The way Cookie was hooking her up that night she was hoping that she would be able to snag her a baller or a quick fix.

When Michelle found at that JaKai was the one who had put her beloved in the hospital she was beyond angry. All she saw was blood she wanted to hurt JaKai so bad for hurting her. Although she hated him so much a part of wanted to ask JaKai why. Because she knew it was so much more to the story. It all didn't seem like something JaKai would do. She knew Cookie was only telling her half of the story but she couldn't question her loved one. Instead she took what she told her and was going to get to the bottom of it, no matter how much Cookie told her to mind her own business and let her or the police handle it. In Michelle's eyes, Cookie couldn't handle her own that's why her ass was up in the hospital for so damn long fighting for her life. JaKai did a number on her ass.

"Thank God for a second chance! Chileeee." Cookie said as she threw her long weave behind her ears.

Michelle nodded her head agreeing. She grabbed her wine glass and poured her a bit of the sweet red wine. She wasn't fooling no one. Damn near everyone around her knew that she was still turning up and drinking more than a pregnant woman should be doing. Not to mention from time to time she would even take a few hits of some good weed. Since she had become pregnant one would have thought she would settle down and sit her ass down a bit. But that wasn't happening at all.

Once Cookie got done touching up Michelle's make up, Michelle stood up and slid into the short baby doll dress. Staring at her stomach in the mirror you could see a little pudge, nothing too big, just looked like she over ate a tad bit. She usually would hide her stomach with her belly band but tonight she felt too damn lazy to dig through her closet to get it.

She stared at her reflection in the mirror. Her makeup and hair were popping.

Cookie quickly ran the wand curlers through her long Brazilian weave. Her makeup was already made up to perfection, all she needed was a little touch up. When she was done, she slid into her leather catsuit, half the right side was cut out, showing off her thigh, lots of leg and part of her stomach area. She slid into her peek toe red bottoms.

"DAMMMMNNN BITCH!" Michelle batted her eyes, Cookie was looking bad as fuck.

"Let's go kill something tonight and put these hoes to shame!" Cookie cracked a pearly white smile.

Michelle high fived her and the two left out.

They pulled up to club Love and the line was thick as hell. But that didn't mean nothing. If anyone knew Cookie, they knew that Cookie didn't do lines. Even with damn near three months out of commission Cookie still had mad pull. Walking up to the front of the club, entrance was granted without any questions asked.

They had just sat down in their VIP section all eyes were on them. Cookie caught the attention of a fine ass nigga and didn't waste no time in going to introduce herself, leaving Michelle sitting by herself.

Michelle ordered a few drinks, sat back, crossed her legs and sipped on her drinks taking in her surroundings. Her eyes lit up when she saw that familiar face in front of her. She couldn't believe that this motherfucker had the nerve to be out in the club partying with his bitch.

CHAPTER 17

Luke, Taylor, JaKai and Nia all pulled up to Club Love. Luke didn't want Taylor out in the club while carrying his child, but with her nagging and nagging about staying home alone he decided to take her. That particular night he made sure he was extra strapped and he also brought along six of his extra men for the extra security.

Taylor had on a BodyCon high waist skirt which was pink, a cut out black crop top and a pair of six inch black heels on her feet. Her hair was pulled up into a tight ponytail, with her baby hairs perfectly flowing freely on her face. Her face was lightly done in makeup, with hot pink lip stick coating her lips.

Nia on the hand had on a tight for fitting BodyCon dress, which hugged every curve she possessed. Her ass was looking extra scrumptious and juicy with the little black fabric hugging the life out of her curves. She wore a pair of hot red Jessica Simpson heels on her feet. Her hair was hanging bone straight down to the middle of her back, with a part in the middle. Her makeup was flawless. You would have thought she had a professional makeup artist do her up.

JaKai had on a pair of Seven jeans, a white tee shirt, a New York fitted on and some black Jordans on his feet, nothing too fancy.

Luke had on a pair of black Prada's on his feet with a matching black Prada linen outfit. His gold chain wrapped freely around his neck, his Rolex was blinging, his fade was fresh to death. He looked extremely sexy, not that he always didn't.

Soon as the group got situated into their VIP section hoes were already flocking like bees to honey as if they didn't notice that half the men in their crew had their significant others with them.

Luke began ordering bottles. That night he wanted half of DC to know who the man on the streets with if they already didn't know. He ordered the damn bar out, treating everyone in the VIP section.

Niggas and bitches was big happy!

Taylor was playing in her phone, when her song came on 'Nan Nigga, by Trina and Trick Daddy.' She placed her phone on the table and stood up and began bouncing her ass and moving her hips to the music.

Luke was deeply engaged in a conversation with one of his clients, Nia and JaKai was hugged up talking to one another.

Nia looked over at JaKai and noticed how he was trying his hardest not to look at Taylor while she was dancing. Looking down at his midsection she could see his manhood quickly growing. She picked her glass of wine and began to sip on it. Her blood was boiling. Either JaKai was attracted to Taylor which a blind man would have been attracted too her as well. Or JaKai was up to no good. The more Nia sipped on her drink the more her conscious began to play tricks with her.

JaKai would take a quick look and hurry and turn his head.

"I'll be right back." JaKai whispered into Nia's ear. Nia nodded her head as she swallowed her red wine.

She looked at Taylor and was becoming a bit envious of her friend. She grabbed Taylor's phone from off the table. Dialing JaKai's number, she checked to see if there was any messages or recent calls in her phone from him. But there wasn't any. Since JaKai and Taylor had their talk at the hospital, they didn't have any communications with one another since. All of JaKai's text messages and any communication with him, Taylor had been got rid of the evidence.

Nia started to question herself. Realizing that she was tripping and that her friend would never betray her. She stood up and joined Taylor and began dancing with her.

*****

Cookie was on the floor getting her groove on with some fine ass chocolate dude who was all into her. It was obvious that he didn't know that Cookie was a man. Had he known he would have beat the life out of Cookie. Cookie haven't had any action in months. Normally she would have told him what the deal was but being that she was desperate for a man's touch she wasn't telling him shit. Not to mention he was splurging on her all night. He had already bought her 3 bottles of Dom P. which her ass drank down like a fish drinks water.

Cookie was tipsy as hell. Her high tolerance for alcohol could have took another bottle or so before she was officially drunk.

Cookie thought she was tripping when she saw JaKai walking past and going towards the bathroom.

She cursed herself out when she realized she didn't bring the small little hand held 380 that she had purchased just for JaKai's ass. The police were taking their good ol' time finding JaKai. He wasn't at none of the addresses they had on record for him and they were barely putting in effort to find him. So Cookie was going to take things into her own hands.

"I got to go to the little girls' room. Stay here, I'll be right back." Cookie told the hunk she was dancing with. He nodded his head and watched Cookie backside as she disappeared. He had to admit the bitches in the club were bad that night but none of them had shit on Cookie, who was flawless from top to bottom.

Staring at her backside he grabbed his jumping dick in his pants. He was definitely hitting that tonight.

Cookie approached the bathroom and took a deep breath. Her mind roamed back to the last time she approached JaKai and the turnout was obviously not the best.

Reaching into her shoulder clutch, she pulled out her brass knuckles and placed them on her hands.

She looked around before entering the bathroom. Peeking her head in she saw a pair of feet under the stall and another man coming out.

"Sorry thought this was the ladies room." She said to the drunk that was passing her.

Seeing no, one else was in the bathroom she bent her back a bit and cracked her neck. Shit was about to get ugly.

Turning around, she was just about to lock the door. Until she felt a pair of strong arms wrapped around her neck.

Little did she know JaKai was waiting on her ass. He wrapped his arms tightly around her neck. Bending her back, so damn far she thought he was about to break her back. He flipped her over on her back. Hovering over top of her, he sent a punch straight to her throat. Cookie began to cough and choke on her own saliva.

"Motherfucker you must want to die!" JaKai said through gritted teeth.

Cookie's eyes blanked a few times as tears formed in her eyes. She knew she fucked up and prayed that JaKai didn't kill her. JaKai yanked her to her feet by her long weave easily. Since being in the hospital she had lost an incredible amount of weight.

JaKai slung her little ass across the bathroom like a rag doll. Cookie body roughly hit the cold floor. Walking to her, JaKai sent three kicks to her stomach.

He wanted to kill her but the knocking at the bathroom door wouldn't allow him to.

He yoked Cookie up off the floor. "Now get your ass up out of here."

Cookie could barely move and felt like her heart was about to stop on her. Yet she quickly got herself together. Embarrassed, she left out the back of the club through the emergency exit. JaKai had gotten the best of her yet again but she promised herself the next time she seen him it wasn't going to be pretty.

CHAPTER 18

Michelle was good and drunk and had her eye on her victim. Finally, she mustered up enough courage to approach him. She stood up and pulled her hair behind her ear.

"LEO!" She yelled directly in his ear, standing behind him.

She looked at the female that was standing arm to arm with him and rolled her eyes.

The female looked Michelle up and down and rolled her eyes as well.

Leo turned around and stared Michelle up and down.

"WHAT!" He spat annoyed as hell.

Michelle placed her hands on her hips." Don't fucking what me. Where the fuck is my ten grand at?" She asked.

Leo burst out into laughter. If Michelle didn't get the fuck out his face he was going to show her where her ten grand was.

"I'll stop by later." Leo told Michelle.

Michelle laughed. "Are you fucking serious. Here you are spending my shit on this hoe! I want my shit now!" She said loudly.

Leo turned around and ignored her. Michelle didn't like that one bit.

She grabbed Leo by the back of his collar. Leo quickly turned around and wrapped his hand around Michelle's neck. He didn't give a fuck about her because the bitch didn't have shit else to offer him. JaKai wasn't fucking with her no more so it wasn't like she could lead him to him. The bitch was broke, hopeless, a headache and most importantly useless in his eyes.

His blood was boiling. "Get the fuck out my face and out my space bitch!" He told her.

Michelle bit her lip, she was about to say something but Leo cut her ass straight off. He leaned in close to her and whispered in her ear.

"Bitch you are fucking useless. I took your fucking money. Me and your cousin Streets broke into your fucking home and robbed your ass blind! I came and fucked you that same night and took whatever else you had left. There's nothing with us, you crazy ass bitch."

Michelle eyes lit up with pure hurt and hatred. She blanked her eyes back to fight the tears.

Leo crushed her entire heart and as for Streets, when she seen him, he was going to be a dead ass motherfucker. When she thought back to the situation, the voice was well too familiar, plus she hadn't heard from Streets since the day he snatched her purse.

Michelle turned around and ran out of the club. She looked up at the VIP section, seeing Nia and Taylor standing there dancing made her sick to her stomach. She then thought about it, JaKai ass was nothing but a dog ass motherfucker. He was fucking both of the beautiful females she saw standing there.

Running to her car, she slipped and fell on her ass, ripping the entire right side of her baby doll dress.

"FUCK!" Michelle cried as the people standing outside began laughing at her clumsiness.

Michelle made it to her car, where she broke down and cried her heart out.

She started her car and pulled out the parking lot like a mad woman, almost hitting a group of people. Jumping on 95 North, she drove like a bat out of hell. Her vision was blurred by the continuously tears, flowing from out of her eyes.

She wasn't just pushing the pedal to the medal going a furious 105 miles per hour, she was also swerving.

She grabbed her cell phone and punched in Luke's number. When the phone rung the first time she realized she had called JaKai. She quickly hung up and thought of Luke's number, which came right to her.

She was going to let Luke know all about the bitch who he was loving and most importantly about the nigga who he trusted so much and thought was his best friend. Hell her life was miserable and fucked up and she was going to make sure everyone around her life was the same. Her blood was boiling, being angry was an understatement. If she had the power she would have killed every being on the fucking earth. She thought back to the time she had caught the girl in her closet. She couldn't believe how trifling JaKai was. And Nia thought that JaKai loved her. She smiled because what came around sure as hell was going to go around. Her mind was all over the place. She then thought about Streets, her own flesh and blood and the way he set her up and betrayed her. FUCK FAMILY. Family wasn't shit. She had something for his ass as well. And as far as Leo, he thought that he was going to get away with what he had done to her. She had something for his ass too. By the time she got done with all the mother fuckers that betrayed her, they were going to wish they were dead. Truth to be told, she was vexed, scorned, fucking crazy and hell hath no fury like a crazy ass bitch who was scorned.

Michelle didn't once look up at the road, not noticing that she was all over the place while still pushing the pedal to the medal. When Luke didn't answer, she let out a loud scream. Determined she redialed his number again. She had plans on blowing up his damn phone until the answered her. By all means he was going to know about his little bitch and his no good ass best friend. She was hoping that Luke would handle JaKai and that Nia would handle her best friend. Leaving all the dirty work to the foursome who was prancing around like there was no care in the world.

"Hello!" Luke yelled over the loud music.

Michelle smiled and looked up at the road but it was all too late. WHAM! She swerved off the road and ran into a police squad car who had a drunk driver pulled over on the side of the highway.

CHAPTER 19

Cookie scanned the parking lot and noticed she couldn't find Michelle's car anywhere. She called her a few times and didn't get an answer. She could believe Michelle had run off and left her. Then again she knew her sister was miserable and when people were miserable there was no telling what they would do. Cookie's red bottoms clicked the pavement as she started walking down the street to catch the nearest cab home. She felt like shit, her first night out she got her ass kicked again. Then got left by her sister and had to leave her dick back at the club. She was just at the corner from the club when an all-black Mercedes Benz pulled up on her. Cookie started strutted hard as hell.

"Aye you!" The driver rolled the window and peeked his head out.

Cookie stopped for a second. Smiling, she turned around and leaned her head inside of the car. The driver was fine as fuck. There was no way she was turning that opportunity down.

"What's up?" She asked him.

"You." He said, licking his lips.

Cookie already knew what the deal was. She didn't mind a little foreplay and a little fun. It was exactly what she was looking for.

When Cookie reached for the door handle, Leo was all smiles. He was happy he found something sexy as hell to get into. Being that Michelle had scared his other bitch away with all the fussing, causing him to put his hands on her.

Cookie got into the passenger seat, reclined her seat back a bit and crossed her legs tightly. Leo took a quick glimpse at her small waist, perfect plush lips and nice sized breast. Her face was angelic and damn when his eyes landed between her thighs and seen her fat kitty poking out from between her tightly closed legs. He damn near lost it. Little did he know it was Cookie's mandingo poking from between her thighs. He was more than pleased with his late night come up.

Cookie was so turned on from the way Leo kept staring her up and down and licking those sexy lips of his she couldn't help but get a hard on. Something had to give. She quickly thought about her needing to snatch her a baller or make a quick come up so she could hurry up and get the sex change that she dreamed of getting. To make her more official than ever. Hell with the sex change it would hard for any man to guess whether or not she's a man.

He drove through the city of DC and ended up getting on the 95 South ramp and going out towards Alexandria, Virginia. He started renting a nice lavish condo back when he had stolen Michelle's money from her.

Before going home, he stopped by a liquor store and then the gas station to grab some condoms.

While Leo was in the car Cookie grabbed her cell phone and started to call Michelle.

She punched her number in and was sent straight to the voicemail after one ring. She then looked down at the phone and noticed that it wasn't her phone, it was Leo's. Curiosity came over her, when she went through the text messages and saw messages from months prior from Michelle and Leo. Anger overcame her when she thought back to the horrible stories Michelle told her about Leo. She quickly put his phone back and pulled her out, When Leo got in the car, he handed Cookie the Big Red gum that she had asked for.

He pulled off in the night and in ten minutes he was pulling up to his condo.

Walking into his condo Leo didn't waste no time at all. They didn't even make it through the door before he started pulling at Cookie's clothing trying to strip her down to her birthday suit.

Cookie slowly pushed him off her. "Can we drink and chill first?" She asked.

Leo smiled but as soon as they sat down he was back at it again.

Cookie pushed him off of her. "Slow down buddy." She told Leo.

Leo laughed, going into his pocket he pulled out his goodies and laid them across the table.

Cookie turned her nose up, watching Leo snort a few lines of coke.

"Wheeww!" Leo squealed holding his nose and holding his head back. He did a few more lines, and laid back. He was on cloud nine. He reached over and began massaging between Cookie's thigh. Cookie squeezed her thighs tightly.

"I have something to tell you." Cookie said to Leo.

Leo sat up and looked Cookie up and down.

"What, you're a man?" Leo laughed. Seeing the humor in his own joke, he burst out into laughter.

Cookie sat up. "I'm a man." She said in her deep baritone.

Leo head spun around so quick. He gazed around the room to see if they had company.

Cookie grabbed her brass knuckles out of her purse and eased them onto her hand.

"Nigga you heard me!" She roared.

She stood up, snapping her neck back.

She sent one blow to Leo's nose, instantly breaking the bridge.

"Yeah, Michelle said what's up." Cookie laughed.

Leo's jaw dropped damn near to the floor. He tried to stand up but Cookie sent a hard kick to his upper chest. The sharp red bottom heel, struck his chest so hard it felt like it ripped through his flesh. He fell back onto the couch.

Cookie jumped on his ass and began beating him senseless. Her hurt and anger was finally released. Hurt from how her parents disowned her, hurt by what he did to Michelle. Hurt by what JaKai did to the two of them. Unfortunately, Leo was the unlucky motherfucker that night.

Cookie had made her mind up. Jumping up on the back of the couch she straddled Leo shoulders, locking her legs tightly around him. She squeezed, squeezed and squeezed the life out of Leo. Standing up she freed him and his lifeless body fell over. She ran his pockets and went through his house taking everything she wanted. Feeling empowered like she was the ruler but more so that bitch at the moment she left. She took his car back to the city and dropped it off. She wanted to be a never kiss and tell type of bitch, but some shit she just couldn't hold. She couldn't wait to tell Michelle what she did for her.

CHAPTER 20

Since Streets had been home, Alesha had been sneaking around with him. She made all types of excuses to her mother so she could get out of the house. Her mother hated the fact that her daughter was creeping and she knew it. But she just couldn't hold her teenager hostage no matter how much she tried to do so. But she did let Alesha know that she better not had ended up pregnant again. And as petty as it was she made sure every morning that when Alesha woke up that she took her birth control pills.

Alesha laid in Streets' arm, staring out the window, lost in her own thoughts. She loved Streets but part of her wanted her youth life back. She wanted to do things that other teenage girls her age was experiencing. House parties, skating rink parties and things of that sort. Every little bit of freedom she got was spent with Streets. He was becoming possessive with her and very aggressive. Lying in bed she had made her mind up. After that night she was going to go about her business and let Streets go. He was just too old for her and she just wasn't ready to settle at that moment.

"What you thinking about?" Streets asked Alesha wrapping his arms around her.

For the past few days she had been acting different and he didn't like that shit one bit. He just knew it was one of them high school boys that she was fucking around with.

Alesha shook her head. "Nothing." She lied.

Streets stood up and grabbed his boxers. Putting them on, he eyed Alesha's cell phone that rested on his night stand.

"Nothing huh," He smacked his gums and picked the cell phone up. "Huh unlock this shit." He told her.

Alesha looked at him like he was crazy. When Streets aggressively grabbed her by her arms, she took the phone and unlocked it for him to go all through her privacy.

First stop was her Facebook, he went through all of her messages, notifications, comments and anything else he could find. Some of the shit he didn't like but there was no sign of her cheating in there. He then started going through her text messages.

Luke: 'I love you.'

Alesha: 'I love you more.'

Luke: 'Nah never, I love you more big head.'

Alesha: 'Shut up when am I going to see you again? You are always with her, now you forgot about me.'

Luke: 'Aww don't say that you know you're my number one. How about a date night next weekend?'

Alesha: 'Sounds great :-)'

Reading the text messages Streets was furious. There was only one nigga named Luke and just the thoughts of Luke taking his woman made him sick to the stomach.

He went through Alesha photos, seeing a picture of Alesha and Luke hugged up. He lost control.

Alesha stood up and was pulling Streets shirt over her head to go to the bathroom. She hated that Streets was acting all nuts and going through her phone. But she didn't care she didn't have anything to hide. Since the two of them had been seeing each other she hadn't so much as look at another nigga.

She licked her lips and still tasting him on her lips she smiled. All the bumping and grinding and screaming and moaning, gripping the sheets and orgasms. She sure as hell was going to miss them.

Just as she got the shirt over her head, WHAM!

Streets knocked her in her mouth.

Blood splattered from Alesha's mouth and she grabbed it. Her eyes were wide open. She was so afraid as she looked at Streets in shock.

"What the fuck!" She cried, backing into the corner.

"You ain't nothing but a fucking little whore. Just like rest of these bitches out here!" Streets yelled.

"I didn't do nothing." Alesha protested.

Streets came towards her. He yoked her up by her throat and slammed her onto the bed. Wrapping his hand around Alesha's neck he stared her dead in her eyes.

Their eyes locked and the coldness in his eyes made Alesha's skin start to crawl. She never saw Streets in such rage. She had a bad feeling that things weren't going to be good for her.

Tears rained down her cheeks because she didn't know what the hell she did wrong.

She thought about leaving Streets but had yet attempted to do so.

"Give me my fucking shirt you fucking whore!" Streets yelled, ripping Alesha's shirt off of her.

Alesha cries became loud and piercing.

"HELP!" She screamed on top of her lungs.

Streets began banging her in her mouth. Her mouth swelled up so big it was ridiculous.

WHAM! WHAM! WHAM!

He beat her all in her face.

"I'm sorry." Alesha cried. Not knowing what she as apologizing for.

Streets looked in her once innocent eyes, raising his fist at her again. He was ready to knock her lights out until his bedroom door swung open.

"JOHNATHAN WHAT IN THE HELL IS GOING ON IN HERE!" His mother screamed. She flicked on the lights. The sight of Alesha and her beaten in face broke her heart into a million of pieces.

She rushed over to Alesha's aid.

"Thank you." Alesha barely mumbled. She snatched the blanket off the bed, Streets tried to grab her but she quickly broke loose from him and fled out of the house. Alesha ran until she was at a gas station. She thought about calling her mother, or calling Luke. Attempting to call both she didn't get an answer. Fearing that Streets would come for her and perhaps kill her she called 911.

Less than ten minutes later, police rushed into the gas station. Seeing the young girl's face, they wanted the bastard who did the damage to her. Alesha got into the police car, rode down the street with them and directed them to Streets' house. Minutes later Streets was being brought out in handcuffs. Walking past the car Alesha was in, their eyes locked with one another.

Streets stopped in his tracks and tears ran down his cheeks. He couldn't believe he did Alesha the way he did her. All he wanted to do was love her and for her to love him equally. Truth to be told she was the only female he ever loved and would be the only female he ever had a chance to experience love with.

Crushing his heart, Alesha banged on the window. An officer opened the back door for her.

"He's my brother Johnathan." Alesha cried.

Streets held his head down. He fucked up, fucked up big time. He knew now he was a dead man.

CHAPTER 21

"No no, it was an accident." Michelle cried. She couldn't believe her luck. She had run off the road trying to call Luke, hit a police car and another car. Now she was being yanked out of hers. Thankfully she was able to make it out of the accident with nothing but a scratch on her face. Her car was flipped up with all four wheels up in the air. One would have thought she was dead for sure seeing the damage of her car.

"Do you need medical attention?" The officer asked Michelle.

He shook his head. He could smell the terrible stench of alcohol oozing from her pores. Not to mention Michelle could barely walk. That accident should have sobered her ass up quick but it didn't.

Michelle rolled her eyes. "No I need to fucking go home!" She snapped.

The officer laughed. "You ain't going home tonight." He said.

He placed Michelle on the curb. He knew with the handcuffs on that she wouldn't go far.

He called in for two ambulances. He was thankful that he was still up and walking. Had he not jumped out of the way he would have been dead, leaving his wife and two precious daughters behind.

He went to go check on the other drunk that he had pulled over, whose car was pushed slightly against the guard railing. He couldn't believe how his night was going. He looked up at the sky to check and see if it was a full moon or whatnot because it sure as hell seemed like one with all the chaos and bad luck he had been through. He noted that the first thing Sunday morning he was going to attend church, because it was the grace a God that saved him.

"Sir are you okay?" The officer yelled approaching the car.

He looked in the backseat for the first time and noticed a car seat. His heart began to beat at a fast pace, snatching open that back door he sighed when he found that the car seat wasn't occupied.

"Sir are you okay?" He asked again approaching the driver door.

He snatched the door open and the driver was slumped over to the side.

The officer thought he was sleep. "You have to be fucking kidding me." He said, shaking the driver.

Noticing that he wasn't moving, he panicked.

Just as he was pulling him out of the car, the two ambulances pulled up.

It wasn't until Michelle got to the jail when she found out that she was being charged with murder. The guy back at the scene was pronounced dead on arrival. To make matters even worse she was charged with a DUI, Reckless driving and picked up on charges that JaKai had pressed against her which was Attempt Murder.

Hearing her charges Michelle damn near collapsed. She grabbed her stomach before letting out a loud pitched scream. This can't be life, she thought to herself.

She was finger printed and booked but luckily she was able to get a bail review right away.

She prayed that her she was able to get bailed out, which wasn't happening. The judge had lost her seventeen-year-old son to a drunk driver two years prior. She was a mad woman and couldn't accept the fact that some worthless bastard decided to make a poor decision and drink then get behind the wheel which led up to them taking her son's life. Not to mention she was an advocate and participant in the MADD group (Mothers Against Drunk Drivers). She shamelessly shook her head at Michelle in disgust.

"NO BAIL!" The judge screamed, banging her gavel.

Michelle's mouth flung open.

"Your honor, I'm pregnant, Please." Michelle shouted out.

The judge stared Michelle up and down. She couldn't believe what Michelle was saying. Women like Michelle made her ass itch. They were trifling and pathetic and in her eyes they didn't deserve to be a mother.

Michelle was pregnant, drinking and driving. Not just jeopardizing her life but jeopardizing the life of her unborn and someone else's child as well.

Meanwhile she prayed and prayed that she could have her son back. She would have given up her own life, just to for her son to have his back. She was sick to her stomach. She had to get up and leave the courtroom before she lost control.

Michelle was taken to the hospital for medical attention. After they checked on her and the baby, which both were fine, Michelle was taken back to the jail.

Reality sunk in when she heard the clinking of the cell doors closing. She burst out into tears and a loud pitched scream which could be heard all throughout the jail released from her mouth.

Michelle went crazy. She had completely lost all control and started throwing herself around the cell. Then she yanked the paper thin mattress off of the bunk.

"I JUST WANT TO DIE!"

"I JUST WANT TO DIE!"

"TAKE ME NOW! OH GOD PLEASE TAKE ME NOW!" She screamed.

She grabbed the sheet from off of the floor. She wrapped it around her neck as tight as she could. Climbing up the bunk she tied it tightly. She was just about to hang herself until a guard burst into her cell. He quickly untied the sheet and restrained Michelle.

Thirty minutes later she was taken from her cell to a different part of the jail, where she was stripped down to her birthday suit, placed in a strait jacket and thrown into an empty cell. That's where she would be spending the rest of her stay.

CHAPTER 22

Taylor woke up bright in early in the morning. Her stomach was cramping bad as hell, not to mention she felt like pure shit. She thought it was gas pain. Since she had gotten pregnant she had terrible gas pain. She leaned over and kissed her sleeping king on the cheek. She grabbed her phone and went into the bathroom. Sitting on the toilet she broke out into sweats, something didn't just feel right. Taylor reached between her thighs.

"LUKEEEE!" She screamed at the top of her lungs. Her hands were covered in dark red blood. Her head started to spin.

Hearing Taylor screaming so loud, Luke immediately jumped up. He looked at Taylor's empty spot and saw that the sheets were soaked in blood. His heart dropped and he prayed it wasn't what he thought it was.

He rushed into the bathroom. Taylor was sitting on the toilet shaking with her hand covered in blood.

"What is this Luke?" Taylor asked him.

Luke shook his head. He was praying that it wasn't what he thought it was. No pregnant woman should be leaking that much blood. Taylor stood up and blood ran all down her thighs. She looked in the toilet and damn near passed out.

"Luke!" She cried.

She fell into Luke arm's. He loved her so much he didn't mind all the blood that she smeared all over his shirt.

He helped Taylor take a quick shower. He carried her out the house and to the car. He drove like a bat out of hell to the hospital. He didn't give a fuck about anyone else on the road. All he gave a fuck about was Taylor and his unborn.

Later at the hospital they found out that Taylor had a miscarriage.

Taylor laid in the bed, slumped in misery. She could barely look at Luke. For the first time in her life she seen a grown man cry. For the first time in Luke's life he shared his tears with Taylor. It hurt him like hell to see Taylor in so much pain and to lose the child that he loved so much in as little as three months. He was looking forward to being a father and to have a family with Taylor.

The upcoming weekend after he took his sister out he was going to take his family and friends out to dinner where he was going to propose to Taylor. Everything was crushed. His high hopes, his wishes and his dreams.

Taylor curled her legs up and swallowed the lump in her throat.

"Luke we can try again." Was all she said.

Luke face was in his palms. He was lost for words and didn't know what to say to Taylor. After a few moments of silence, he got up and sat in the bed with Taylor. He wrapped his arms around her and kissed the nape of her neck.

"I love you, we will try again." He told her.

Taylor thoughts were all over the place. She didn't understand what she had did wrong. In her eyes she felt like God was punishing her but she didn't know exactly for what. She prayed she wasn't being punished for what she had done with JaKai. All of her life she had always been a sweet, innocent young girl. She felt bad for what she had done to Nia. She thought about just coming clean and telling her the truth. In fact, she had to tell Nia and Luke the truth. She couldn't continue living a lie. The truth was going to set her free but not at that moment.

She laid her head against his rock hard chest. She broke out into a heavy cry. So heavy that it had a powerful impact on Luke and it lead up to him crying. He held Taylor tightly in his arms and the two of them cried together.

CHAPTER 23

Nia woke up bright and early to the fresh smell of bacon, eggs and her favorite French toast being cooked. She quickly hopped in the shower then made her way downstairs.

JaKai's sexy ass stood over the stove cooking for her. She became wet seeing that all he had on was her apron. She stood back and admired his sexiness. He was so damn fine. Since she had left the hospital she didn't have to go back home to her mother. JaKai purchased a nice size three-bedroom house located on the outskirts of Washington DC. She was thankful for him and more than grateful for everything he had done for. Shortly after he purchased the house for her he bought her a brand new Nissan Maxima. He opened a bank account for her, placed nine thousand and five hundred dollars in it and brought her an entire new wardrobe. Doing more for her than anyone ever done.

She walked up to him and wrapped her arms around him. She grabbed his dick and began stroking it until it was hard as brick and was poking out of the apron.

"Mmm." JaKai grunted.

Going in front of him, Nia dropped down to her knees. Pushing the apron to the side she stuffed his dick in her mouth.

Loud slurping sounds could be heard over the frying of the bacon. She took his dick deep into her mouth. Her warm mouth tightly wrapped around his dick. Pulling it out she spat on the tip of it then stuck it back deep down in her throat. JaKai threw his head back well satisfied with the sloppy toppy that he was receiving. She was sucking his dick like she never done before. If all it took was a little breakfast for him to experience a mind blowing treatment like this, then he was cooking Nia freaky ass breakfast every damn morning!

"FUCKKKK!" JaKai moaned, Nia wrapped her jaws around his dick tightly, sucking and squeezing the life out of it. JaKai lost control and skeeted all down her throat.

JaKai knees were so damn weak from the powerful nut he had just released down Nia's throat. He pulled out a stool from their kitchen bar and sat down on it.

Nia hopped up on the bar and threw her legs up in the air. She pulled her panties down, lie back on the counter and spread her legs.

Her thighs shook and cream filled JaKai stuck his hand in her hot pie.

"Ohhh." She moaned.

Since she had gotten pregnant she was always more wet than normal and freakier than a motherfucker which was a big plus for JaKai. He had no complaints at all. She was satisfying all of his needs and for once he didn't even think about cheating on Nia. As far as he was concerned there was nan bitch out there that could top what Nia was offering. She was bad as hell, could cook her ass off, kept the house clean, didn't ask for much, could suck a mean dick and had some good ass pussy. All the shit JaKai adored.

He lowered his head and in return he gave Nia the best head ever. One thing about him was that he specialized in multi orgasms.

"OHHH JAKAI! I LOVE YOU! I LOVE YOU!" She cried loudly. Her thighs were wrapped tightly around his neck. She couldn't contain herself she knocked over all the contents off of the bar top.

JaKai flipped her over on all fours, he placed his fingers underneath her softly stimulating her clitoris before he entered her.

He fucked her so damn good, Nia couldn't help but let out cries of joy and thank God in the process.

JaKai let loose his semen deep into Nia's wet pussy.

"I love you." He said out of breath.

"I love you so much." Nia cried.

"Good," JaKai slapped her plump ass, "Bring that breakfast upstairs and cut that oven off. A nigga is tired." He huffed.

Nia shook her head, climbed off the bar, turned the stove off, fixed her and JaKai's plates and met him upstairs to their bedroom.

CHAPTER 24

Nia quickly scarfed her breakfast down. She laid across the bed flicking through the channels on her sixty-four-inch television. She turned around.

"JaKai, have you been honest with me about everything? " She suddenly asked.

The question threw JaKai off guard. He shoved the bacon in his mouth.

"What's up?" He asked Nia.

Nia turned the television off, got up and sat down next to him. Propping her leg up on the bed she faced him and stared him deep into his eyes.

The other night at the club and the way JaKai was trying his hardest not to look at Taylor didn't sit right with her. Not the mention when he was able to steal a look at her, the look was a different look. It bothered her and he had to know the truth.

"How many times have you fucked Taylor?" She asked.

JaKai looked at her like she had two heads.

"Never." Rolled off his tongue.

Nia was silent, and stared at him for a few seconds. She wanted to believe him but something just didn't feel right.

"Okay, if you say never then I believe you." She said. She took a mental note. JaKai never asked her what would make her say something like that or anything of that sort. He was too damn calm. She knew a liar when she saw one. Although she was hoping that she was wrong. She glanced down at her cell phone.

"Well she texted me this morning. Get dressed so we can go see her. She's in the hospital." Nia said.

JaKai nodded his head, playfully nudged her and leaned in for a kiss. "Lil butt you really be tripping." He told her.

JaKai got up and went into the bathroom. The entire time he was thinking he should have told the truth. He hated to lie to Nia. He was releasing his bladder when Nia walked in behind him.

"If I find out you are lying." She shook her head, grabbed her makeup bag and left right back out of the bathroom.

JaKai waved her off. He was good, Taylor wasn't going to tell on herself and he was going to be sure that Nia didn't ever run into Michelle again, or so he thought.

They arrived at the hospital. Nia was hurt when she found out that Taylor had a miscarriage.

JaKai and Luke was staring out the window discussing some important business.

Nia leaned close to Taylor.

"Was it JaKai's?" She asked Taylor who was sipping on her apple juice.

Taylor damn near choked. She faced Nia and stared deep into her eyes. She didn't know rather JaKai's love dizzy ass ratted the two of them out or if Nia was onto something. At the club she had caught Nia going through her cell phone but she didn't question her.

"Are you fucking crazy?" Taylor smacked her gums.

Nia stared at Taylor. "I'm sorry." She said and stood up. She very well felt like shit.

"I'm sorry for your lost Luke. I'm sure in no time y'all have y'all bundle of joy." She said.

She leaned over and kissed Taylor on her forehead. Taylor was staring at Nia awkwardly.

"JaKai, we have to hurry for my appointment." She told him.

JaKai gave Luke dap and the two of them left.

Nia felt bad for presenting the drama to Taylor while she was laid up in the hospital but she just couldn't contain herself. Something was just irking her soul.

Later that day while she was in the house cleaning up she heard a loud knock at the door.

Looking out the window seeing that it was a sheriff she debated whether should she answer the door or not. Going with her gut she answered the door and was handed a paper with JaKai's name on it.

Closing the door, she read the paper. It stated that Michelle was picked up on her warrant that JaKai had put out on her and his next steps on what he would need to do with his case.

Nia hand traced the paper, lost in her own thoughts. She should have left well enough alone but she just couldn't do so.

*****

Michelle was surprised when she was directed to the visitation area. She sat down and impatiently waited by the jail's phone. She had no clue who was visiting her but she prayed it was God, delivering a miracle for her. Because with the charges she had, she knew her life as over and most likely they would throw the book at her. Being charged with murder just didn't sit well with her. She couldn't believe that she had actually killed a man.

She attempted on pulling her hair back behind her ears to somewhat look a bit presentable. But that didn't do the job. She looked a hot fucking mess. It was going to take a flat iron and a bag of makeup to bring her back to life. Her past couple of days had been shitty and her looks proved it all. When she saw Nia glowing with her little belly bump and coming toward her she was sick. The beautiful girl was her reminder of why she was in there and why her life was so fucked up. It was her young hot ass who was the root of all her problems. Even more anger consumed Michelle. Her blood was boiling and her heart was racing very fast. At that moment she made sure she was going to break Nia down so bad and that she too was going to feel how miserable she was. She wasn't going to be the only bitch walking around pregnant and miserable.

Nia's visit only last four minutes in which all four minutes caused her an incredible amount of pain and heartache. She wished she would have never visited Michelle. She ran out of that jail so damn fast. Her shirt was drenched in her tears. Seeing her rush out in such a mess, Michelle temporarily felt satisfied. She gave Nia exactly what she was looking for. You go looking for trouble that's exactly what you would find. Especially fucking around with a scorned crazy bitch like Michelle.

CHAPTER 25

When Michael found out where Michelle was he was beyond frustrated. Then for her not to have a bail he was even more upset. Michelle was all he had. Their first visit together he felt so bad for her. He couldn't believe that she had killed a man. She looked so shitty. He wished the jail would have allowed her to bring in a makeup bag so she could give Michelle a quick make over who was in desperate need of it. Cookie promised Michelle that she wasn't going to leave her hanging and she was going to fight with and for her until the very end. After that visit, Cookie had been trailing JaKai damn near every day, marking down all of his moves. She didn't have the strength in her to serve JaKai his punishment at that moment but seeing him and Luke carrying in the duffle bags into the trap, she made her best decision. KARMA WAS A BITCH…

*****

JaKai and Luke had woken up early in the morning to get to their business. Their first stop was the docks where they picked up their connect's last of supply for that week. Luke played the music on low and took his time driving back to their trap. The last thing he wanted to do was to get pulled over with ten bricks of cocaine, well hidden in his tire.

They made it to the trap safely. Luke went inside first and u and got it situated. Minutes later JaKai had loaded the bricks up into a duffle bag and was carrying it into the house.

They sat at the table cutting the coke up and just conversing with one another.

JaKai took a sip of his Corona and listened to Luke who was schooling him.

"We been grinding, all summer, all winter long, getting no sleep and barely eating. Our investments are bringing a good cash flow in. I say that we give this shit a few more runs then after that go on to a better life." Luke spoke.

JaKai shook his head. He gave it a thought or so but he wasn't expecting it all to be so soon. He had been broke before and he'd be damn if he ever went back to that life. He had bad spending habits and once before he had a bad gambling habit. Needless to say he didn't have as much money as Luke, not anywhere close to it. He knew Luke was good but he wasn't. And he couldn't accept a grown man taking care of him and Nia. That shit just wasn't going to happen. Luke could very well throw his towel in but he wasn't ready to do so at the moment. Until he got where he needed to be he was going to trap or die in the process of trying to trap. He wanted to make sure that he was financially secured.

"So soon?" JaKai said.

Luke looked down at work. Something wasn't right about it. Licking his pinky and dabbing into the coke. He then stuffed his pinky in his mouth. No effects, no nothing. Placing his head to the table he couldn't believe the shit. THEY HAD BEEN RIPPED OFF. Over two hundred thousand dollars were thrown down the drain.

Pissed off Luke grabbed the other bricks and busted them open. All of them were the same. He tasted it again and couldn't believe he was tasting baking soda.

Luke didn't have to say anything. JaKai already knew what was happening.

"FUCK!" JaKai cursed. Standing up he knocked the table over freeing all its contents.

Luke grabbed his phone, swung the bathroom door open and walked outside. He was so heated he needed a walk. He called his connect and couldn't believe the number was disconnected. Determined he called all four of his numbers and they all were disconnected. Luke's blood was boiling. He couldn't believe what had just gone down. After over a decade of fucking with a motherfucker and he decided to suddenly get cute and test Luke. Blood was going to shed and somebody was going to die.

*****

JaKai was inside of the house pissed as hell. He was hoping that Luke was getting things situated. He suddenly started to get a weary feeling. He walked toward the window and couldn't believe his eyes. Squad cars pulled up in front of the house. JaKai hit the back door and was ready to bounce. Three officers attacked him and threw him onto the ground. His Miranda rights were read to him and he couldn't believe that he was being arrested for the attempt murder of Cookie. He wished he would have killed that motherfucker that day in the bathroom when his ass decided to test him. Yup he should have been a dead motherfucker that day. On the upside JaKai was happy that they had got ripped off and the coke was fake. Had it been real he would have been going down for a long time for sure.

*****

When Luke saw the police, he already knew what time it was. He tucked his phone in his pocket and got the hell out of dodge.

*****

Seeing JaKai being put in handcuffs Cookie was well satisfied. She started her car and pulled off.

CHAPTER 26

Nikki stepped out of the shower and pulled her wet hair into a tight ponytail. She snatched her robe off of the toilet and wrapped her body in it. She walked back to her room and was sickened with the pathetic man lying in the bed. Last night's sexcapade was more than life itself. But she was just upset with the mere fact that the motherfucker was wearing out his welcome. She walked into her bedroom and immediately woke him up and dismissed his ass.

Sitting alone in her house, she looked around. Thoughts of Nia consumed her mind. She was still somewhat affected by what had happened to Nia. After doing her homework she found out that Michelle was arrested which she was doomed about. She wanted to make that bitch pay for what she did to her daughter. Nonetheless Michelle had a mother, a father and a brother that was still prancing around town like they had no worries in the world. One of them motherfuckers were going to pay for their daughter's actions if not all of them.

CHAPTER 27

Nia kept ignoring JaKai's collect calls. She didn't have any words for him. She went back to their house and began packing her shit. She couldn't believe that he was playing her. Looking in full length mirror at her growing belly, she broke down in tears. As bad as she wanted to she couldn't hate Taylor as much as she wanted too. A part of her still loved her best friend and she just wanted to know why. She turned her cell phone off and got dressed in a pair of Pink by Victoria Secrets sweat pants, a matching top and a pair of her all white Jordans. She fixed her hair into a high bun and brushed her baby hairs down.

Getting in her car she drove to Taylor's house.

She knocked on the door and seconds later Taylor came running to the door.

"Hey girl." Taylor cooed, opening the door for Nia to enter.

Taylor didn't even see it coming. WHAM!

Nia knocked her dead in the face. Nia ran into the house and slammed the door behind them.

Taylor grabbed her face and looked at Nia.

She didn't say a thing. She knew exactly what that punch to the face was.

Nia grabbed her by her hair and threw her up against the wall. Pictures fell onto the floor. Nia roughly slung her across the circular living room table. Shit was all over the floor. Needless to say, Nia mopped the damn floor with Taylor's ass, pregnant and all. Taylor not once fought her back, not just because Nia was pregnant but more so because she knew she deserved that ass whipping.

Nia whipped her hair back out of her face and stood over Taylor who was defenseless and lying there.

"Why the fuck did you have to fuck my man! Out of all of the dicks around here! Why fuck JaKai!" Nia screamed at the top of her lungs. Standing over Taylor she looked like a mad woman.

Taylor cried and shook her head, "It happened before you and him and one time after you two were together. I don't know what I was thinking. I'm so sorry Nia. I'm so sorry."

Nia wasn't trying to hear that shit. She began kicking Taylor in her side.

"IS THAT ALL YOU HAVE TO SAY HOE!" She kicked Taylor in her side. "BITCH YOU WAS SUPPOSE TO BE MY BITCH. WE WERE BEST FRIENDS. DID ANY OF THAT SHIT MEAN ANYTHING TO YOU? YOUR TRIFLING ASS FUCKING MY MAN AND HIDING IN CLOSETS AND SHIT. BITCH YOU ARE FUCKING TRIFLING!" Nia yelled, reminding Taylor of the day when she could have very well lost her life.

Taylor didn't know where Nia was getting her information from but she was pretty sure with all the facts that Nia was stating that she must have gotten it from the horse's mouth, either JaKai or Michelle. She cried her eyes out and wished she would have just told the truth.

Nia was tired of Taylor sitting there sobbing. She pounced on her ass and started to beat the brakes off of Taylor's ass. She was far from finished. She had planned on camping out at Taylor's and Luke luxury home and beat Taylor ass until she was fucking tired.

The front door opened, Luke walked in and couldn't believe the two best friends were fighting.

He rushed towards the two of them and yanked Nia off of Taylor. Wasn't no bitch about to get the best of his girl.

"What the fuck is going on in my fucking house?" Luke furiously spat.

Nia looked Luke up and down with evil eyes. “Ask your fucking HOE!” She spat.

She grabbed her car keys and left Taylor there to explain to Luke all about her hoeism.

CHAPTER 28

"What the fuck is she talking about?" Luke asked Taylor.

Taylor didn't bother getting up off the floor, nor to turn over and face Luke. The truth was out. Like they say what happens in the dark will always be brought to the light and all of her and JaKai's dirty secrets were brought to the light.

Taylor began crying and her heart was aching terribly. She had just lost her best friend and was possibly losing her man.

She laid there covered in blood, sobbing heavily.

"What the fuck is all of this about?" Luke asked Taylor, nudging her.

He helped her to her feet. He was already having a horrible day and was hot about getting ripped off and to make matters even worse his trap was raided and JaKai was arrested.

He didn't have time for the games Taylor was playing.

He grabbed Taylor by her chin, forcing her to look him dead in his face.

Taylor blinked her tears away.

"Nia found out that JaKai and I had messed around." She nonchalantly spoke.

Luke couldn't believe his ears. Before he knew it, he hauled off and smacked Taylor across her already aching face. As soon as he slapped her he felt bad. He knew JaKai was a dog ass motherfucker but never expected him to be so low, but then again he couldn't be so mad after all. His thoughts roamed back to when Michelle had given him that sloppy toppy, which didn't make him any better than JaKai.

But as for Taylor on the other end, he had her placed on a high pedestal.

He couldn't even look in her face, she made him sick. He thought she was different but come to find out, she was just let the rest of the females walking around.

"The first time it happened was the night I met you at the club. Yeah my nasty ass let him fuck me in the girls' bathroom. The second time it happened was when you left me at his house with him. I don't know what the fuck I was thinking..." Taylor said.

She started to tell him the whole truth but she didn't want to tell him that she fucked him in the hospital as well while she was pregnant with supposedly his child.

"The baby, who did it belong to?" Luke questioned.

Taylor blanked her eyes.

Luke coldly stared at her.

"Thirty days and I want you out of my house and out of my life bitch." He said disrespecting Taylor how she had disrespected him and more importantly herself.

He walked out of the house, leaving Taylor there to herself. Taylor broke down in tears. Although she didn't have anywhere to go that didn't matter to her. What mattered to her was that she had just lost her better half, her best friend, her parents and her child.

Luke had given her thirty days but she decided she would get out of his hairs before then. She couldn't tolerate the fact that she hurt him so bad when she promised him that she would never hurt him. She walked up the steps and into their bedroom. She grabbed three of her oversized suitcases out of the closet and began packing her things. Going into one of Luke's safe she took five thousand from him in all which she was going to pay him back.

She left the car behind and caught a taxi to the nearest hotel. On her ride to the hotel, she looked out the window and broke down into tears again. Luke was all she knew and all she wanted to know. Nia was her best friend, her sister. She now had nothing all over dick. She was going to find her a small apartment and find her a job. Her eighteenth birthday was approaching and it was time for her to get on her grown woman shit.

CHAPTER 29

Nia pulled up to the jail, walking in with her Gucci bag hanging from her side. She appeared to be a bad bitch so after whipping Taylor's ass, she went home got cute, grabbed some money to bail JaKai out. She packed up all of her shit and put it in her car. Her mind was made up, she was leaving JaKai's trifling ass and she took majority of the money he had in the house. She sure as hell wasn't going to leave him empty handed. He was going to pay for all of her pain and suffering.

She walked into the jail and paid JaKai's cash bail which was two hundred fifty thousand. A part of her didn't want to pay JaKai's bail but she figured she would do that so she could comfort him.

Two hours later JaKai was walking out the jail. He was so happy he was a free man. He smiled when he seen his beautiful lover sitting on the hood of her Nissan Maxima.

When she saw JaKai approaching her, she got into the car and started it up.

"Damn baby I miss you and my unborn so much." JaKai said getting in the car trying to hug Nia.

Nia fought back the tears. "YEAH THAT'S WHAT YOUR FUCKING MOUTH SAY. WAS YOU SAYING THAT SHIT WHEN YOU WAS FUCKING MY BEST FRIEND!" She yelled.

WHAM! WHAM! She knocked JaKai upside of his face.

She didn't give JaKai a chance to speak.

She pounced on his ass and began beating the life out of him.

"WHY YOU FUCKING DO THIS TO ME KAI!" Nia screamed. JaKai couldn't duck the hits, Nia's punches were so damn hard.

"Man I know I fucked up Nia. It only happened twice." He lied.

"I DON'T GIVE A FUCK HOW MANY TIMES IT FUCKING HAPPENED YOU DUMB ASS! THE SHIT SHOULD HAVE NEVER HAPPENED!" Nia spat. "OH AND WHILE YOU WAS SO BUSY FUCKING MY BEST FRIEND, YOUR BOY WAS BUSY FUCKING MICHELLE!" Nia laughed.

JaKai couldn't give two fucks who Michelle was screwing. The bitch was a hoe so he didn't expect much from her. But thanks to Nia for the valuable information. That was something that he was going to bring up when he met up with Luke. In his eyes it was all fair game, an eye for an eye. You fucked my bitch and I fucked yours, is how he felt.

She opened the passenger door and climbed off of JaKai, "Get the fuck out you dog ass bastard! I gave you chance to be honest with me!" She yelled.

JaKai looked back at Nia. He had really fucked up. Looking back in the backseat he saw all of her bags. Nia put the car and park and damn near ran JaKai's feet over pulling off so fast.

JaKai backed up against the curb, he was going to let Nia have her space but it wasn't going to be for too long. He just wanted her to cool off. He watched Nia fly down the street and disappear around the corner. He grabbed his cell phone and called OnStar and turned the GPS on, Nia was out of her fucking mind if she thought she was going to leave him. He already knew he fucked up and it was time to face the music with Luke. It was time for him to man up and be a man about the shit that he had foolishly done.

CHAPTER 30

Luke sat as his mother's kitchen table while he waited for her to fry him some chicken.

She turned around and looked at her son.

"You look like you just lost your best friend. Is everything okay?" His mother asked, sensing something was wrong with him.

Luke held his head low.

"Fuck both of them." He muttered. He looked down at his phone and noticed that it was JaKai calling. He didn't have shit to say to him at the moment. Instead he sent the call to the voicemail. Had he talked to JaKai or met up with him like what two grown ass men was supposed to do, JaKai would have been floating down someone's river.

When his mother got done cooking, she placed Luke's plate in front of him. Grabbing the hot sauce, she poured it all over his chicken just how he liked it.

"If you love her, follow your heart. If JaKai's really your best friend, forgive him. I'm not saying be a fool, but we are humans. As humans we all make mistakes and I'm sure you made plenty of them." His mother coached.

Luke shook his head and slightly cracked a smile. He couldn't believe his mother knew what was going on. Just as a mother should. No one knew their child best like a loving and caring mother.

Luke took a bite of his chicken. As he was feeding his face, Alesha walked into the kitchen. It had been a little over a week since Streets beat her up, but her bruises still looked fresh.

"What the hell happened to you?" Luke barked.

Alesha grabbed her face. “Some hating chicks from school.” She said. The same lie that she had told her mother when her mother questioned her about her face.

Luke raised his eyebrow. Since the last big lie Alesha had told it was hard for him to believe much she was saying. He seen all the sneaking and hiding that she was doing around the house, he was no fool.

“Yeah and you better have left that motherfucker. When I find out the nigga who put his hands on you, he’s dead. In fact, his entire family is dead.” Luke threatened.

Alesha looked into Luke’s eyes. She sat down on the table and grabbed his hand. Her big brother loved her to death, every word he spoke she believed. “Luke it was girls from my school.” She told him.

Luke nodded his head but he wasn’t buying that shit. Alesha wasn’t the type to be in any drama. She kept to herself and nonetheless bitches knew not to fuck with her.

Alesha looked down at her ringing cell phone. It was Streets calling her. Since the day he went to jail he had been calling her nonstop. But she didn’t have any words for him.

Later that night sitting on his mother couch, Luke started to miss Taylor. Everything about her he wanted. He wanted to hate her but he just couldn’t as much do as so. He didn’t have to question could it be love or not, he for sure knew it was love. Without Taylor his heart was aching.

He called her cell phone, and was upset when she didn’t answer. But that was fixed when his phone rung seconds after he had hung up and it was Taylor calling back.

Luke got her location, raised up from his mother’s couch and started heading out towards the door.

Alesha coming down the steps stopped him in his tracks. Laying across her bed she had so much to think about. She tried to figure out if she loved Streets or if it was fiction or whatnot. She kept questioning herself and deep down, despite what he had done to her she had to admit that she loved him. Although she wished there was some things that he would have changed. Like all the aggressiveness, then there were the trust issues, and invading her privacy. She truly missed all the good times that the two of them shared. When she was with him, he made her feel like she was the only girl in the world. He did things to her and for her that she never experienced before. Being the first time ever experiencing those things gave her an incredible rush like no other... Not just that, Streets protected her and would never let anything happen to her. He uplifted her, he encouraged her to stay in school, and to stay focus. He wasn't just her lover, her man but he became her best friend as well. She didn't know what sent him over the edge that night but clearly it was insecurity that sent him into the state of a madman. She had started to write him numerous of times but wasn't able to fulfill that attempt. She thought the words but just didn't know how to pen them on paper without becoming angry. Her aching face, reminded her to hate him although she barely had any hate in her blood.

So instead she decided to pick Luke's brain. Her big brother seemed to have the answer to answers and that the solutions for everything.

"Luke do you believe in second chances? Do you believe in giving the one you love a second chance?" Alesha asked.

Luke looked up at his little sister, "I believe everyone deserves a second chance, some even deserve a third chance. But don't be no fool." He recited the words which once a wise woman had told him and that wise woman was his very own mother.

"Thank you." Alesha softly spoke.

"But if that nigga put his hands on you, you better second guess that shit. Because if a nigga put his hands on a female once then he would do it again, it's now in his blood." Luke advised her.

He then thought about how earlier that day he had placed his hands on Taylor. He was being so judgmental and a hypocrite, because he promised himself that he would never get that angry again and lay hands on Taylor. No matter what she did in his eyes no woman deserved a man putting their hands on them.

He got silent then took his words back and went with his first statement. "Well I can't say that you'll never know if a person will change or not. We are all humans and we make mistakes. Some learn from them some don't. Some are truly sorry some or not. So yes, I believe everyone deserve a second chance, some even deserve a third chance. But PLEASE don't be no fool.

Alesha nodded her head, "I love you Luke." She told him.

Luke smiled, "I love you more big head." He told her and disappeared outside of the door.

Luke arrived at Taylor's hotel room. She opened the door dressed in a soft pink baby doll dress. He could tell that she was crying all day due to her puffy eyes and the redness around them.

He wrapped his arms around Taylor.

Taylor laid her head against his chest.

Luke closed the door behind him, picked Taylor up and carried her to the bed.

Taylor was so thankful that Luke had come around sooner rather than later. She missed her baby so much and it hadn't been an entire day that the two had separated from each other.

Luke stripped Taylor from all of her clothing. She ran her soft hands all over his physique body.

Their eyes deeply fixated on each other's.

"I'm so sorry Luke." She cooed.

Luke spreader her legs far apart. His tongue flicked over her clitoris. He took two fingers and mounted them deep inside of her sugar walls.

"OHHHH." Taylor softly cried.

Her juices rained all over Luke's tongue. Luke tongue fucked her until her legs were shaking and she couldn't bear to take anymore. He turned her over and pushed her down on her stomach. Removing his pants, he climbed on top of her and penetrated her from the back.

"OHHHH LUKE! I LOVE YOU! I LOVE YOU!" Taylor cried, Luke was fucking the life out of her, taking her to a sexual measure at its greatest. He was for sure leaving his mark all in her pussy. When he got done beating Taylor's pussy out of the frame she was going to never think about another man again. Her sexual punishment he was putting on her she was already regretting that she fucked JaKai in fact the dick. He was so good; she didn't have any records of JaKai at that moment. JaKai who? Too bad that those memories couldn't fade away from Luke, he busted his load all inside of Taylor. When he got done he got back dressed. Taylor fell onto the bed, out of breath, with a super wet and throbbing pussy. She turned around just in time to see Luke walking back out the door.

"LUKE!" She screamed jumping up from the bed. She grabbed the sheets to cover her naked body and rushed out the door to chase behind him.

She caught him just in time to see him get on the elevator.

"I LOVE YOU!" She yelled after him.

Luke looked up at her and their eyes locked. He didn't say a word. He got on the elevator and walked out of her life. No matter how bad and how much he wanted too, he just couldn't find forgiveness, at least not at that very moment.

CHAPTER 31

Late that night Luke met up with JaKai at a local bar. He hesitated before going inside. Murder was on his mind but then at the end of the day JaKai was his best friend, the two were like brothers. Then he thought about it, he was the damn fool for leaving his girl with JaKai knowing how JaKai was. So there was no one to blame but himself. Although JaKai was wrong as well.

Luke shook off the ill feeling and walked into the bar, he found JaKai sitting front and center. Looking at him boy he could tell that he was a bit down. Luke walked up to him and grabbed a seat beside him. He ordered his normal, double shot of Henny and coke.

"What's up nigga?" Luke said.

JaKai shook his head, "Man the power of pussy." He shook his head then threw his drink back.

Luke shook his head, "The power of pussy. I caught the toppy from Michelle and you fucked my bitch. I don't know what went down with you and Taylor but shit else better not ever go down or I'ma kill both of y'all motherfuckers and then plan a nice burial." Luke said. He tapped JaKai on his back and from there was understood didn't need to be explained. Luke spoke his final words and JaKai took heed to his final words.

Luke got up and disappeared out of the bar.

He went back home. He couldn't even get any sleep. For one he wasn't use to sleeping without Taylor and for two Taylor was blowing his phone up so much he was forced to cut it off.

CHAPTER 32

Alesha lifted her head from the toilet where she had been sick the past three days. She came down with a terrible cold. Her mother suggested that it might have been the flu. Alesha was agreed with her, because she knew there was no way she could have slipped up and got pregnant again. She was on birth control and didn't think it was possible. Still she wanted to check and be positive. She pulled out the home pregnancy test which she had purchased from the Dollar Tree. There was no use in her wasting money on an expensive test, those dollar store ones work as fine as all the other higher brands.

Sitting on the toilet she spends on the test and crossed her fingers that it was negative.

Unlucky her, those two red lands popped up and stood attention. Alesha couldn't believe what the hell was happening to her. She broke down in tears, her first thought was to get an abortion but then she thought who she almost lost her life from the last abortion. She hid the test, ran into her room. She threw herself on the bed and threw her face into her plush purple pillow.

"Why! Why! Why!" She cried her eyes out.

Standing up in the mirror she absorbed her belly, looking a bit closer and actually paying attention to her stomach. She realized that was no longer flat as a surf board as it usually was that she in fact had a bit of a pudge. She tried to guess the time Streets had been gone and the time they messed around. She came up with her being at least eleven weeks pregnant if she was doing the math correctly.

Alesha thoughts were all over the place, she then made her final decision, she was going to keep her child, be a damn good mother but in the meantime hide her pregnancy. She figured she might as well not show up to her court date as a witness to Streets' case. They hoped that all the charges would be dropped and just maybe him and her could co parent and do what was best for their unborn.

CHAPTER 33

Months later…

Nikki was finally ready to punish motherfuckers. To muster up the courage all it took was three blunts and numerous amount of shots. She sat at the bar drinking and thinking to herself. The more she drunk the more influenced she became. She stared into her purse and fiddled around until her hands came across the nine millimeter gun that she had bought off of the streets months ago. She ordered one last shot of E&J then got up and left out the bar. It was always that cheap liquor that would have a motherfucker feeling investable like they were Superman or some shit. Nikki wasn't in her right state of mind but then again her mind was already made up. She had been plotting for months and was finally ready to do what she promised herself she was going to do. She drove all the way out to Michelle's parents' house, and killed the lights in case there was anyone outside they couldn't witness her in that area. Pulling up a few houses down from their house she turned her car off. Not giving what she was doing any thought she eased out of her car and slowly closed her car door. She crept to the back of their house, and damn near jumped out of her skin when she seen the lady wrapped in her robe standing outside. She looked further into the yard and noticed that she was letting their dog out for a late night run. The lady walked further into the yard, when she got far enough, Nikki eased into the house. She ducked off in the living room closet. Standing in the closet she couldn't believe what the hell was going on. She began touching herself and realized that she left her gun and her purse in the car.

"SHIT!" She cursed.

A few seconds later she heard the dog running in the house.

"No you're not going upstairs buddy! You know where your home is." Michelle mother screamed. She opened the basement door where they apparently kept their dog. The dog turned around and ran down the basement steps. She closed the door behind him and locked up the house. When Nikki heard her walking up the steps she came out the closet and followed her up the steps. Michelle's father was in the bedroom sound to sleep.

Nikki stood at the top of the steps, as the bedroom door closed. Her mother disappeared inside. Just as Nikki was about to walk up to the door, it flung open. She quickly stood behind a tall wooden stand. Michelle's mother headed towards the steps, Nikki quickly jumped out.

"Hush." The lady grabbed her chest and breathed deeply.

Nikki rushed towards her, pushing her backward. She lost her step and before Nikki knew it the lady fell over the banister. She had come there to punish someone but didn't know it was going to happen like so and be so easy.

She looked over the banister and noticed the lady legs went bent so far back it was touching her neck, which was turned sideways.

Nikki covered her mouth because she couldn't believe what she had just done.

"Shit!" She covered her mouth.

Hearing the loud noise, Michelle's father jumped up from out of his sleep. He rushed to the closet and grabbed his shot gun.

"WHO'S THERE!" He yelled cradling the shot gun.

Nikki turned around and before he could come out off the door she rushed down the steps and the old man was right on her ass.

Nikki hit the front door, swinging it open she ran across the neatly manicured grass. At that moment she regretted that she went to Michelle's parents' house, then broke in their house unprepared at that.

She was running across the grass like a damn track star then all of a sudden. BOOM!

Michelle's father fired the shot gun.

"AHHHH" Nikki screamed in agony. The bullet hit her right in the back of her shoulder. Ripping her flesh apart. Tears ran down her cheeks.

BOOM!

He shot her again. Nikki felt like she was going to pass out and die but she wasn't giving up. She made it to her car, through blurred vision, started her car and pulled off.

BOOM! BOOM!

The back windows were shot out. Neighbors now rushed out of their house from all the shooting. Nikki drove down the street like a bat out of hell. She made a sharp right, minutes later she was getting on the highway. She was fighting for her life and trying to spare at it the same time.

She drove thirty miles out until she found a hospital in Alexandria, Virginia.

At the hospital she was treated and two days later, with her IV in her and all she fled from the hospital, hitched a ride and was getting the hell away from Washington DC.

CHAPTER 34

Cookie sat in the living room of her parents' house. She couldn't believe what she was going through. Late the night before her father called her, hearing the hurt and pain in his voice she just knew something wasn't right. Her stomach was turning and her head was spinning. She didn't know how she drove to her parents' house but she did. When she got there, seeing the paramedics and all of the police cars her heart instantly dropped. When she saw the morgue carrying out the black bag she knew it was only one person. Her mother…

"NOOOOOO!" She let out a loud pitched scream. She fell to her knees and grabbed her stomach.

Her father rushed out of the house, hearing his child's loud cries. He helped Cookie off the ground and helped her into the house.

Cookie dropped her head into her palms.

It took her a few minutes to get herself together. She lifted up her head, "Daddy what happened?" She finally asked.

He sat down beside her, and rubbed his hand softly across her back. "I don't know, there was an intruder in here. Your mother and him must have gotten into a fight. She threw her over the banister. I shot that motherfucker two times! I hope she die a slow and horrible death." He said through gritted teeth.

Cookie turned to face him, "She?" she asked.

Her father nodded his head. "Yes it was a woman."

"Did you see what she looked like?" Cookie raised her eyebrows. She couldn't see who would come to her parents' house and do any harm to them. They didn't bother anyone. Her mind was all over the place.

"No." He shook his head, he dropped his head in his palms.

"I don't know how to tell Michelle this."

Cookie shook his head, "Let me handle this."

The next day when Michelle was delivered the devastating news she was beyond heart broken. Another nightmare added to her already life filled with nothing but nightmares.

"Are you kidding me?" Michelle asked.

Cookie reached her hand out and touched the glass window that separated the two of them. Michelle raised her hand and placed it up against the window in front of Cookie's.

"Mommy is gone, I'm in here. My entire life is fucked up. I don't know what I'm going to do anymore. I just don't want to live." She said to Cookie.

Cookie understood just how she felt, she too felt like giving up on life. Feeling as though life had given up on her. But she couldn't let Michelle know that. By all means she had to uplift her sister and continue being her backbone. Her sister was in desperate need and needed her help.

"Well you can't give up! You have me to help get through life and most importantly you have that beautiful baby boy who will need his mommy." Cookie told her.

Michelle shook her head, "I don't have anyone, I'm in here alone. They'll take my baby then who do I have."

Cookie got quiet and stared at her sister.

"And you better be a damn good parent to my son, there's no way I'll let JaKai and that bitch ever get my child." She told her.

Cookie shook her head, "I'll be a damn good father to him."

Michelle raised her eyebrows, she didn't know what Cookie meant by she would be a good father but she didn't question her either.

The following week later, Michelle didn't attend the funeral. There was no way she would be able to hold up and see her mother tossed in the ground.

Instead she laid butt naked in her cell crying heavily.

Cookie's father was surprised at the funeral when he seen his child there dressed like a man. For the sake of his nephew Michael had made the decision to be the best man and father he could be. He threw all of his makeup, all of his woman clothing and shoes and all of his feminine products away.

It was a tough task. The night prior he prayed on it, prayed on it, got on his knees and prayed on it. The next morning, he woke up with the decision of getting a life back that part of him wanted.

CHAPTER 35

Taylor sat on the toilet and couldn't believe the results. She was pregnant yet again. It kind of broke her heart that Luke wasn't there for her to share the news with him. In fact, she didn't have any way to contact him. It had been months and she still didn't have a number on him. He would call her from private numbers, talk to her for hours and when she would get comfortable he would end the call. She hated that she had broken his heart. And for Nia, Nia still wouldn't answer her either.

Taylor pulled out another test and pee'd on it as well. She then thought about to the last time she was touched by Luke. He had fucked her so damn good, it was still thick on her mind like it had happened the night before. That was months ago, so she figured she was a couple of months pregnant. She couldn't wait to go to the doctors and find out how far along she was and seek the proper medical attention so the same wouldn't happen like it had happened before. She grabbed her phone and had to text someone the good news. She started to text Nia then stopped. Instead she kept her good news to herself.

*****

Nia sat on her couch in her own crib, which she gladly purchased with JaKai's money. She was in her last trimester and had tuned the entire world out all expect for Nikki. Sitting on the couch with her legs spread her stomach touched the brim of the couch. She was so damn fat and tired of being pregnant yet she wasn't complaining. She hadn't told anyone about her secret but Nikki. Her fourth month going into five-month checkup she had grown larger by the seconds. Her stomach was feeling a lot heavier and she just knew something wasn't right. Well that day she found out that she wasn't only carrying one child but two. She didn't know if she should have been happy or scared, regardless she cried both tears of fear and tears of joy. The only person that knew was Nikki. She didn't plan on keeping it from JaKai that long but the day she gave birth he was going to be hella surprised. Her and Taylor have talked or spoke, the last time she had seen Taylor was the time that she was pounding her face in. She had to admit, she missed her best friend. Not just her best friend she missed her man, but she was stuck in her stubborn ways and wasn't ready to forgive the two of them just yet. Both were still calling her until that day but she didn't answer. If she really wanted them out of her life, she would have changed her number or blocked them but she didn't. Truth to be told everyday she looked forward to the two of them calling her and telling her how sorry it was. It was pathetic as hell but she appreciated their gesture of trying to amend things and rekindle their relationships/friendships.

She got up and went to the shower. Stripping down to her birthday suit she looked at her reflection in the mirror. She couldn't wait until she had her babies so she could get back into the gym. She felt so damn fat and ugly although she was so beautiful and glowing. Thinking of JaKai she started massaging her nipples. She was so wet between her thighs, like she was every damn day. She was seconds away from breaking down and calling JaKai. Instead she returned to her room, she pulled out her bullet and sexed the hell out of herself. After two orgasms she went back to the bathroom and got in the shower. The hot water bounced against her body, suddenly a sharp pain ran from her stomach to her back. Nia took a deep breath and grabbed her knees, the sharp pain came again. Feeling wetness between her legs she looked and noticed the tub was red.

"OH SHIT!" Nia yelled. She hopped out of the shower and thought of who she could call. She first called Nikki, whom she hadn't heard from in over a month. She thought she could do the labor thing alone but then when time came she didn't want to be alone. She needed her friends and her man there.

"TAYLOR I THINK I'M IN LABOR, GET YOUR FUCKING ASS OVER HERE NOW!" Nia screamed over the phone to Taylor. She gave Taylor her address and Taylor was more than glad to assist.

Taylor made it to Nia's house in less than ten minutes. She helped her best friend into the car.

Nia breathed heavy between the powerful contracts.

"FUCK! FUCK! FUCK!" She screamed.

"TAYLOR I FUCKING HATE YOU WHY DID YOU DO THIS TO ME!" She screamed.

Keeping one eye on the road Taylor turned to face Nia, "Do what, I didn't get you pregnant?" She laughed.

Nia shook her head, she pulled out her cell phone.

"JAKAI I FUCKING HATE YOUUUUU!" She cried between a contraction.

JaKai didn't know what the fuck was going on with Nia's crazy ass but it felt good to hear his voice. Him and Luke was out tearing the city up, getting money like they did on the normal.

"What the fuck did I do to you now Nia?" JaKai asked.

"I'M IN FUCKING LABOR!" She screamed over the phone.

JaKai stopped everything that he was doing. "I'll be there baby and don't have my baby until I get there."

Four hours later, Nia was giving birth. JaKai stood on one side and held one of legs up and Taylor stood on the other.

Both JaKai and Taylor were shocked as hell when the second baby was delivered.

"What the fuck?" JaKai questioned.

Out of breath and tired Nia rolled her eyes. "Surprise." She smiled.

JaKai couldn't believe it, he was a father. Not to one but to two handsome and beautiful little bundle of joys.

"JaKai Jr and JaNai." He named his babies. Liking how their names sound together he repeated it again.

He walked over to Nia and gave her a kiss on the lips and brushed her hair back out of her face.

Nia smiled, "You better not ever make me leave you again boy!" She said.

At that moment she forgave both Taylor and JaKai.

JaKai gave both of the babies to Taylor. He opened the door and allowed Luke to come in.

"Look at the babies." Taylor cooed.

Luke walked over, looked at the babies then looked back at JaKai.

"Congratulations. They both look like you. Wait why is there two?" He asked, the last time he checked JaKai was only supposed to have one.

JaKai shook his head, "I'm surprised just like you are."

They all burst into laughter.

"No for real, only a few months ago I found out I was having twins. They said it was the hiding twin syndrome. So I'm just as surprised too." Nia admitted.

JaKai jumped up in the bed with Nia and planted kisses all over her face. "Damn thank you lil butt, you just made a niggas life." He told her.

Taylor and Luke handed them their babies, Taylor began taking pictures of them. The Kodak moment was so perfect. The room was filled with love.

Taylor looked over at Luke, she smiled. "Your next." She softly spoke to him.

Luke heart melted, he wrapped his arms around Taylor. "I love you."

"I love you and I miss you Luke." She told him.

The two of them engaged into a deep kiss. At that second Luke forgave Taylor. He missed his love and wanted her back. He knew that it wasn't going to be perfect but it sure as hell was going to be worth it.

CHAPTER 36

Michelle sat in her cell and was hurt when she got her mail. She looked down at the pictures and let out a high pitch cry. The babies were gorgeous. JaKai and Nia seemed to be so happy. She was pissed that she wasn't able to do damage to their love by telling Nia all of his dirty secrets instead she brought them closer and made them stronger than ever. She was pissed that everyone was happy but her. She looked down at her belly and rubbed it. She glanced back up at the pictures and became even more furious seeing that there were two little bastards; a boy and a girl. She turned the picture over and read their names. She lost it, she couldn't believe that some young bitch had beat her to the punch and stole her child's name. Her baby boy was supposed to be named JaKai Jr.

Michelle stood up to her feel and began screaming, yelling and running naked around her cell. She had a fucking fit. The guards had to come in and restrain her. Later that night after being in an incredible amount of pain and a hard labor she gave birth to her son James JaKai naming him somewhat after JaKai being that JaKai name was JaKai James. She looked into his handsome face and he favored his daddy so much. Feeling complete she instantly fell in love. Too bad she would be signing her rights over to Michael and her baby would be taken from her in thirty days. Until then she was going to love her baby boy like no other and when he was gone she was going to continue to love her.

CHAPTER 37

Luke, Taylor, Alesha and his mother all sat at the table and indulged into the delicious breakfast food that she had cooked. The table was covered with foods such as bacon, eggs, grits, hash browns, sausage and French toast.

Luke sat at the end of the table as a king should always be seated at. Taylor sat beside him, Alesha sat across from her and his mother sat at the other end.

Luke looked at Alesha, "Why you got that big ass shirt on?" He asked.

Alesha shook her head, "No reason."

Taylor looked at her and gave her a warm welcome smile. She didn't know why they didn't see exactly what she was seeing. It was obvious that Alesha was hiding something and not to mention the beautiful glow that graced her. It was obvious that she was pregnant but Taylor wasn't saying a thing. It wasn't her business to be all up in their business.

Feeling her stomach turn, Alesha got up and excused herself then rushed off to the bathroom.

After they finished their breakfast, she was still in the bathroom puking her guts out.

Taylor knocked on the bathroom door.

"Who is it?" Alesha yelled.

"It's me Taylor. Can I use it really fast please?" Taylor asked.

Alesha wiped her mouth and washed her hands.

Taylor stood in the door frame, handing Alesha her prenatal pills and her nausea medicine.

"You need to tell someone and you should be seeing a doctor. Hiding it will on make things worse and with all of the lying no one will ever trust you again." Taylor told her.

Alesha shook her head. "I will soon." She replied.

Taylor smiled, "Hopefully before you have the baby." She reached out and touched Alesha stomach and could literally feel the baby kicking.

Alesha smiled. "It's a kicker." She laughed.

Taylor shook her head, "You better tell your family. Like today!"

Alesha crossed her arms. "Maybe next week." She brushed past Taylor and went into her bedroom.

Taylor shook her head and walked into the bathroom. She lifted her shirt up and smiled at her growing belly. She was already into her second trimester. The morning sickness and all she was in love with it. She couldn't wait until the day came for her and Luke to meet their bundle of joy. Speaking of Luke, things have been great with the two of them. He forgave her and never once said a word about what happen. She made a promise to him and herself that she would never forsake them as long as she lived. As for her and Nia they were back at it like nothing never happen. Friends always forgive, not forget but deep down in their heart they find forgiveness.

******

Alesha's phone rung, seeing the familiar number she sighed. She decided to pick the phone up this time. "Johnathan." She softly spoke.

Streets had to take a double look at the phone. These last three months he'd been trying to contact Alesha she finally answered.

He took a deep breath, "Sorry Alesha. Man I snapped out that night. I just want you to know that I love you and I forgive you." He told her.

Alesha smiled, "I love you and I forgive you too." She replied.

"Thanks, I was just trying my luck. I didn't think you would answer. Would you come see me tomorrow?" He asked her.

Alesha thought for a quick second, what harm could it do? After all she had news for him that she would love to share with him face to face. Still confused she bit her nail, "Yes, what time?" She asked.

Streets gave her the time, after hanging up Alesha's thought process lead to whether she was making a mistake or not.

Streets on the other hand was looking forward to Alesha coming to see him. He borrowed his roommate's fresh kicks and got himself together that night.

Alesha fell asleep on top of her sheets. She woke up feeling very ill. She stood to her feet.

"Ahhh!" She cried out.

She looked between her legs and couldn't believe what was happening. The gush of water flooded out of her, then the contractions came immediately afterwards.

"MOMMA! MOMMA!" Alesha screamed on top of her lungs.

Luke, Taylor and her mother was all downstairs watching videos of Luke and their family when they were younger. They all jumped when they heard Alesha screaming.

Luke was the first to burst through the bedroom doors. He rushed to Alesha aid. She turned to face her love ones. "I'm pregnant and I think I'm about to have my baby." She cried…

2 hours later she gave birth to a beauty premature baby girl who was rushed to the baby NICU, fighting for her life. Since she was such a fighter Alesha named her Tiger.

CHAPTER 38

JaKai and Nia came out the court room with their twins. JaKai was so damn happy that Michael didn't show up to court and all of his charges were dropped. He did know that Michael had other plans for him. So in return he was going the same thing with Michelle. Which wouldn't have made a difference in Michelle's case being that she had the murder charge on her and the judge she had, had a bitter taste towards her so things wasn't going to be good for her.

CHAPTER 39

Nia woke up bright and early and pranced around the house. After getting the babies bottles made and getting them dressed she hopped in the shower. She lathered her wash cloth and started washing her body. She felt a set of hands on her, turning around she smiled.

"Thought you was sleep sleepy head."

He grabbed the wash cloth from her, "How could a nigga sleep with all that noise you were making?" He laughed.

Nia shook her head. "I wasn't that loud." She playfully splashed some water on him. She turned around and stuck her face underneath the water.

JaKai stuck the washcloth between her legs from the back, washing her up.

She spread her legs a bit, suddenly she felt his hot tongue in between her thighs.

Leaning forward she held her balance by holding the wall in front of her.

He stuck his tongue in and out of her hot box.

"Ohhhh, you are so nasty." She softly moaned.

JaKai kept licking and licking. His tongue flicked over her clitoris then he would slide it deep inside of her and move it around in a circular motion then pull it back out and flick it over her clitoris again.

"OHHHH DADDY!" She cried. Her leg began to shake and hot cum squirted all over JaKai's face.

JaKai slapped her on her ass, "Hurry up and get ready for work." He told her.

Nia turned around and smiled, "You don't care that I'm going to work?" She asked him.

"Your eighteen now, you're an adult. Do what the hell you want to do woman!" He replied.

Nia shook her head.

JaKai slid back out the shower. He didn't approve of Nia working a job, especially one at the prison. With all the grinding he did and the money they had saved up there was no need for her to want to do anything but look pretty and raise his kids. But she on the other hand claimed she needed to get out before she fell in the postpartum slump.

He gave her a week and knew she would be quitting. JaKai out of everyone knew Nia the best…

Nia walked into the prison and was happy that she finally had her first job. She hated to leave her family behind while she worked but the doctor suggested that she got out and did something with herself other than shopping and getting pampered all day. So she decided to get a job, eight hours a day would do her life some justice.

Nia followed her beautiful trainer around as she introduced her to other staffs and other parts of the jail. She stared at her thick backside and couldn't help but admire her small waist and big ass. She wasn't into girls but she had to give credit where it was due.

"Is that a nursery?" Nia asked pointing.

The girl shook her head, "Yes that's where new mothers spend their first and some last thirty days."

Her and Nia walked over towards the room and looked into the glass window.

Nia shook her head. She became a bit sad, the thought of a mother not being able to raise her kids and leaving them or them being taken away from them in thirty days. She didn't know what she would do without her babies. She watched for a brief moment while the mothers bonded with their blessings and nourished them.

She looked at one woman sitting in the corner who looked like she had been through hell and back. She couldn't believe what was in front of her eyes. She stared at Michelle for a few moments while she breast fed her baby boy who was all wrapped up and bundled in a baby blue blanket. She was dying to see his small little face because she wanted to see if he looked like JaKai or not. The old her wanted to go into that room, sit Michelle's baby in the basinet and whip the life out of her. Since she had become a mother she grew into a much wiser and better person. She couldn't dare go back to the ways or even worse, whip her ass and risk losing her children or anything of that sort. Besides from the looks of things it looked as if life was taking an even crucial ass whipping on Michelle.

Nia quickly excused herself and went to call JaKai. If it was his baby, then it was their baby. She would love JaKai son just like she loved hers. She told JaKai quickly to call his lawyer and order a DNA test.

Nia impatiently waited until later that day when the took the babies back to the nursery. She walked past the nursery searching for the baby. She didn't have to search too long when she seen the baby, her heart melted. It indeed was JaKai's baby. She wished she was able to carry her phone throughout the jail so she could snap a picture of the baby and show JaKai. Nia stood on the opposite of the glass for a few minutes and admired his small handsome face. Tears were in her eye. She was not mad at JaKai at all, Michelle was before her, so she completely understood. She prayed his lawyer could work something out. She would hate to see the precious baby with someone other than his parent, which was JaKai.

The rest of her work day she was in a miserable mood. The thoughts of the baby were all over her mind, not to mention she missed hers and her man. She couldn't wait until her shift was over. When it was she sat in her car and broke down in tears. She was now determined more than ever to do the right thing for the sake of that child.

CHAPTER 40

Words couldn't explain how horrible and sad Alesha felt, after giving birth to her baby who was two months early and not just two months early but was also not growing properly was taken to the NICU it broke her heart. She felt like a failure as a mother. She wished she would have been getting the proper care for her child. Now she had to watch Tiger fight for her life. Her cell phone rung. Seeing that it was Streets calling she sighed.

She listened to the operator then pressed 1 to accept the call.

"Yes." She softly spoke of the phone.

"BITCH YOU FUCKING MAKE ME SICK. ALL THESE FUCKING GAMES YOU PLAYING WITH MY HEART! WHEN I SEE YOUR ASS—"

CLICK!

Alesha hung up on him. She didn't have time for him and his drama at the moment. The only thing on her mind was her child.

She didn't bother waiting for the nurses to help her out of bed. Instead she climbed out of bed by herself. She even made it to the bathroom on her own and released her bladder. She then walked out and made her way to the nursery. Standing there she looked at Tiger who was hooked up to all sorts of machines. She smiled although she was hurt by seeing her baby there fighting for her life. She placed her hand up against the glass.

"Keep fighting Tiger baby, mommy is with you every second. Fight baby girl and never give up." She told her daughter with tears in her eyes. Alesha stood there for at least an hour watching her daughter. She was so in love, with her three pounds and one ounce, head full of hair beauty. Later she was able to go inside, hold Tiger and breast feed her for two and a half hours. Which she loved every second of. When she got released from the hospital she was heartbroken. She missed on late nights going to watch Tiger. She knew her baby girl was going to be home with her in her arms in a few months if not sooner, because her Tiger was a fighter, everyday her progress report was better and better.

CHAPTER 41

Michelle was furious when she was served the papers from JaKai's lawyer for a DNA test. She sat in her cell crying her eyes out there was no way she was going to allow JaKai and that bitch Nia take her child from her and play house with her baby. Over her dead body, too bad with her stay at the prison baby James JaKai was part the prisons property. As Michelle was reading the papers his mouth was being swab. With extra pay, JaKai and Nia ordered a rapid DNA test which they would have the results in three to five. In which Michelle would be signing over her rights to the baby in 3 days to Michael.

*****

99.999 % the test results read. JaKai looked at Nia to see what she had to say. He couldn't read the expression on her face. Nia picked up her son and grabbed the bottle to start feeding him. "Well JaKai, she was before me. I guess you was still dipping and dabbing because her son is the youngest. But that's neither here or there. Let's take the next step in doing what we have to do."

JaKai stared at her. "Are you sure?" He asked Nia.

Nia nodded. "I thought on this, I'm positive JaKai. He's your son and he needs to be right with you if the mother can't have him. It's only right and it's only fair to the two of you." She said.

JaKai nodded his head agreeing. He was going to get his son by any means. "Have you heard from your mother?"

Nia shook her head. "Yes. Only once, she said she was in Atlanta with a friend of hers."

"She still want to be young." He laughed. "Are you going to work?"

Nia stood up and looked at the time. "Hell yeah, let me go get ready. Finish feeding the babies."

She quickly rushed to the bedroom and started getting dressed. She couldn't wait to see baby James JaKai. For some reason she was becoming very attached to that little boy. Soon he would be in her and JaKai's arms and care where he belonged.

CHAPTER 42

Luke and JaKai cruised the streets of DC. Luke jumped on to 95 South and drove out to the Potomac Mall. His mind was made up on what he wanted to do with his life. He had a baby on the way and couldn't believe in a few months he would be a father, now he was ready to really start his life but first he couldn't do so without making things official and have a wife. Later that night Luke had a dinner at his house, which included Nia, JaKai the twins, his mother and Alesha. Smoked salmon, all sorts of fresh vegetables, wild rice and potatoes were served. They all sat at the table eating and enjoying ones another company.

Luke cracked open a bottle of Moet and then began pouring everyone glasses.

"I have a toast I want to make." He stood up.

Everyone got quiet and gave him their undivided attention.

"First I want to thank all of my family and friends for coming out tonight. Secondly I want to make a toast to all of us and to our future. The roads have been rocky but everything is all well worth it." Everyone clinked their glasses together.

Luke walked over to Taylor and helped her stand to her feet. He wrapped his arms around her. With her big stomach touching him he could feel their daughter kicking him. "She never want me touching her mommy." He laughed.

He then got on his knees.

Taylor covered her mouth, she couldn't believe what was happening. "Will you marry me Taylor?" Luke popped the big question.

Taylor fanned herself, tears of joy ran down her cheeks. "Oh my God Luke! Yes! Yes!" She screamed.

Luke slid the rock on her finger, it was so beautiful and heavy.

He stood up and picked her up. Everyone was excited for the two of them.

"She said yes!" He announced to everyone as if they didn't hear her.

Every clapped and cheered them on.

Luke and Taylor shared a kiss that seemed as if it was going to last for eternity. Luke was the happiest man on earth and Taylor was the happiest female on earth.

Luke stared at Taylor, "Since you said yes then first thing Monday morning we are going to apply for our marriage license and we are getting married." He told her.

Taylor was all smiles. She looked at the rock on her hand admiring it. She nodded her head, "Yes anything for you baby." She smiled, her future was so damn bright. Eighteen years old, an amazing soon to be husband, everything that she could ever want and ever need and to top it off her first child on the way. There was nothing else in the world she could ask for but having her parents around. She thought about calling them but it was dismissed quickly, she wasn't ready to forgive them. Especially her father, the way he did her she would never forget. Then her mother didn't give her a call, so in her eyes she was siding with her father. Wouldn't no real woman or mother sit back and allow their husband to beat up her pregnant daughter. So Taylor decided to let them be and let bygones be bygones and move on with life with her newfound, God giving family.

CHAPTER 43

Depression had taken over Michelle; she didn't want to live no more. She felt like she couldn't live. What did she have to live for? Two days before she got the results back and the baby was JaKai's before she knew it they were taking her baby from her. JaKai had rapidly fought for rights and legally since she couldn't care for the child it was given to his next relations which was his father JaKai. Michelle cried and pleaded and pleaded for them not to take her child away. None of that mattered though. Cookie well now preferred to be called Michael was beyond furious. He promised Michelle that he would get his nephew back my any means. To make matters even worse, Michelle was sitting in her cell sobbing, hearing the correctional officer boots hitting against the hard floor she didn't bother looking up until the noise stopped in front of her ceil. A few moments later she wiped her tears and looked up. Seeing Nia's face she damn near lost it. Nia smiled at her.

"Poor tink tink cheer up. Life isn't that bad. Cheer up you little miserable bitch! And for you to ever think you was going to ruin my life you got me fucked up. Now bitch sit in here and rot in hell! Oh and thanks for the beautiful baby boy, he loves eating off of mama's breast!" Nia spat.

"NOOOOO!" Michelle screamed. She charged at Nia but the cell blocked the two of them. Nia backed up a bit and stuck her tongue out.

"KARMA IS A PURE FUCKING BITCH!" She told her.

Michelle broke down screaming at the top of her lungs. Just as she pushed Nia to her limits before now the tables had turned and Nia had pushed her to her limits…

It was the day of her court and she knew the judge was going to throw the book at her. With her mental evaluations she was found to have skitsofrenia, suffered from depression and was also bipolar. She felt like it was the end of the world. Especially how Nia came and visited her, that drove her even more insane, pushing her to her limits.

The two guards pulled to the back of the courthouse, opening the door they began getting all fifteen inmates out of the van and lining them up against the van. Michelle was the third to get out. She squinted her eyes and checked her surroundings. She looked behind them and noticed the highway was not too far from them. Handcuffed and all, she eased off a bit. The guard turned around and noticed Michelle was a few feet away from the van.

"GET BACK IN LINE!" He screamed at her.

Hearing his voice Michelle took off running. The small fence that was there with all her will she threw herself over it. The guard chased after her while the other one called in that a prisoner had escaped. He got the others in the van.

"RUN MICHELLE! RUNNNN!" The others chanted for her.

Hearing them chanting gave Michelle more motivation. She took off like a bat out of hell. Running towards the highway Michelle no longer gave a fuck! She didn't have anything to live for. The guard stood back, there was nothing he could do…

Michelle ran right on the highway. Giving up on everything she stood right there in the first lane. Cars swerved all over the place trying not to hit the handcuffed maniac. It was impossible, one car going a hundred and ten miles per hour, couldn't stop. BOOM! He hit Michelle. She never once blinked. Her petite body flew ten feet in the air, hitting the ground she was hit by another car and ran over top of. Pieces of her body was separated, matter, guts and blood was everywhere.

"OMG!" The guard covered his mouth, the scene was something that no one would have wanted to see. His heart went to Michelle and her family. He covered his mouth and began crying, forever he would remember what he had witnessed today.

Michelle took her own life and died a painful death. Little did she know after hearing after thing the judge felt sympathy for Michelle. She was ordering Michelle to do five years in a mental institution where she could have her child at and raise him for the entire five years there. The father would have been granted custody and the two of them would share split custody. Michelle life was never over, she made her life over.

CHAPTER 44

Taylor gave birth to a beautiful baby girl. Luke cradled the baby in his arms.

Taylor smiled at him, "Did you come up with a name yet?" She asked him.

He looked down at his precious daughter, "Precious." He said.

Taylor smiled again, "Love it baby, Precious it is. How does it feel to be a daddy?" She asked.

"The best feeling in the world." Luke stood up and walked over and kissed Taylor on the lips.

"I have my family. Now I'm complete." He told her.

Taylor nodded her head. "Now we are complete." She corrected him.

******

Alesha was happy as hell, Tiger was doing so good and had picked up the right amount of weight to leave the hospital. Her and her mother went to pick her up and finally she had her daughter in her arms where she wanted and needed her to be. Her mother was doing a great job helping her out in all the ways she could. Alesha sat in Tiger's room and rocked her in the rocking chair while she sung sweet lullabies to her precious baby girl. With her mother's help she was going to finish school, go to college and get a job and be the best mommy to Tiger that she could be.

CHAPTER 45

Alesha didn't expect to get a call from Streets but she did. He was home and was on the streets. He wanted to see her, Alesha gave it some thought, part of her mind was telling her no while the other was telling her yes. She made her mind up on meeting him at his mother's house then thought against it. She decided if she met him in public that he couldn't do any harm to her. So they met in the parking lot in front of a Rite Aid. When Alesha got off of the bus, Streets was already there waiting for her.

Streets' heart melted when he saw Alesha. She had put on some weight and she had matured a bit. she looked more beautiful than ever.

"Johnathan." Alesha spoke approaching him.

Streets smiled, "Can I get a hug?" He asked her.

Alesha stepped forward and gave him a hug, Streets held her tightly into his arms until she pulled away.

Streets got quick to the point, "Do you love me?" He asked.

Alesha smiled, "Of course I do."

"Do you want to be with me?"

Alesha looked down and began fingering the locket around her neck. There was no point of leading Streets on or selling him any pipe dreams.

Alesha shook her head. "I want to focus on school, and get myself together. I don't want to be with anyone at the moment." She told him.

Streets became furious. That wasn't what he wanted to hear, from Alesha getting him arrested, all the broken promises he had enough.

Alesha took one look at him and could tell that he was upset with her. She looked around the parking lot and seen a few cars parked, people were walking on the streets. She backed up a bit.

"I shouldn't of came." She told him.

Her gut was telling her to run and she did just that.

Leaving Streets standing there she took off running across the street like a bat out of hell.

Streets ran after her, Alesha was way too fast for him to catch.

He whipped out his gun… BOOM!

The bullet pierced the back of Alesha head, her body fell lifeless onto the ground.

Streets ran up to her, "Fuck Alesha!" He cried.

He flipped her over and stared into her lifeless eyes. His heart was shattered into millions of pieces.

People on the streets screamed and ran for cover. A madman was loose with a gun and all they thought about was saving themselves.

Streets hugged Alesha tightly then snatched the locket from around her neck. Inside his lungs felt like they didn't have any oxygen. The picture of Alesha and a precious baby girl that looked like he spat her out himself was there. Alesha was just not his lover; she was the mother of his child.

"I'm sorry! Damn Alesha, why you didn't tell me!" Streets cried.

He picked the gun up, lifted it to his head…BOOM! Right in the middle of the streets of DC he killed himself, and lay right next to the love of his life.

CHAPTER 46

Taylor walked out on the patio and stood next to Luke. Ever since his sister's funeral he had been down and depressed. He barely ate and he barely said two words to anyone. Taylor prayed for him and his mother every day and every night. She wished there was something to do to heal both of their pain.

She wrapped her arms around him tightly as her nose filled with his expensive cologne, "Baby you have to come in and get something to eat. I need you to be strong and healthy. Your daughter and your niece needs you."

Luke didn't say anything. "What do you think Alesha would have wanted you to do?" She added.

She grabbed his face and looked him into his eyes. Tears ran down his cheeks. She softly kissed his lips. "Luke I need my husband back and your daughter needs her daddy back, now. I'm going to need you to pull it together."

Luke laid his head against Taylor's shoulders, "She was my baby sister, she didn't deserve what happened to her. I should have been found out who that bastard was and killed him." Luke told her.

Taylor knew exactly how he felt, she too was furious about what had happen to Alesha.

"I know baby, but there's nothing we can do right now, but do what's best for Tiger and our family." She told him.

She grabbed Luke by the hand and led him inside of their home. She sat Luke on the sofa and went and got Precious and Tiger. She sat both in his strong loving arms.

Luke stared at Precious then stared at Tiger who was staring and cooing at him. She instantly touched his heart.

"I love all three of my girls." He said.

Taylor sat down and kissed him. She knew in due time her man was going to be back up and running. She knew her and both of her daughters, being that she now claimed Tiger as hers was going to just fine.

JaKai and Nia were finally happy that JaKai had gotten his second son from Michelle. With a little trickery, she signed her rights over to her father who willingly signed his rights over to JaKai. JaKai and Nia family was now completed. She had her set of twins, JaKai Jr. and JaNai, JaKai's second son James JaKai and her unborn which she was hoping was another girl. JaKai hopped on the highway and got onto 95 South. Nia was in her phone and she didn't notice that they were going away from their home. JaKai had hustled super hard and was able to save up enough money to move Nia and his family out of state into their new home and to open up a business which would keep funds flowing in. Living in Washington DC he wasn't promised another second, the beefing, the hating the drama and the street life were the only that was there for him. He was finally manning up and was doing what was best for himself and his family for once. JaKai pulled up to a gas station to fill the tank up. The entire time him nor Nia knew that they were being trailed. JaKai killed the ignition and leaned over towards Nia and playfully snatched her cell phone from her. "Why you always in that phone? What you stepping out on me?" He asked.

Nia shook her head, "No Facebook is like a drug Kai!" She laughed.

JaKai grabbed her lips with his. They embraced in a romantic kiss. "And you're like a drug to me." He told her.

Nia melted between her thighs, causing her panties to soak with wetness. JaKai's sensual and affectionate side always caused those sort of effects. He was a street nigga but for sure had that thug passion like no other. And the dope dick he slung, was always A1!

He got out the car and went to pay for the gas, then stood outside pumping the gas. He looked into the car and admired his family who he loved so much. When he was younger he always wanted a big family. Now he finally had a big family. His two boys, his girl and another one on the way. Nia and her beautiful self was the topping of the cake. She was everything he wanted in a woman and then some more. She was bad as hell, smart, supportive and always had his back since day one. He was glad that he was able to fight for their love and not lose her. She completed his life and he completed hers. She was soon to be wife but she didn't know it yet.

Once they got settled in their new home he was going to propose to her that night. Seeing if Nia was still into her phone, he reached into his pocket and pulled out the ring. He smiled, she was going to be his wife before she knew it.

He knocked on the window, Nia glanced up at him.

"I love you lil butt!" He told her.

Nia smiled. "I love you more JaKai." She replied.

******

Michael grabbed the gun that was sitting in the passenger seat. He was furious after losing his mother, his sister, his nephew and his damn self. He didn't give a fuck about anyone's life nor his. He got out his car and began walking towards JaKai. "This is for Michelle." He said raising the gun.

Before JaKai even knew, before he could run and hide. BOOM! BOOM! Michael pulled the trigger.

The bullets pierced JaKai's skull. His body fell to the ground. Michael dropped the gun and took off running.

"JAKAIIIIIII!" Nia screamed on top of her lungs.

All of her babies were screaming on top of their lungs. She rushed to the side of the car to see JaKai lying there. Blood was running from his body and he was barely breathing. He laid there fighting for his life, putting so much into the fight, he just couldn't leave his family. Truthfully God had given him more time than expected, with both bullets hitting him in the head he should have been dead one you would have thought.

Nia dropped to her knees and laid JaKai's head in her lap. Through blurred vision he looked up at her.

He wanted to say something but it just wouldn't come out. Nia rubbed her fingers around his face.

"JaKia I love you so much. Please don't leave me." She begged and she cried.

She ran leaned down and kissed his lips. His chest softly heaved up and down. Nia went into his pockets, grabbed his phone and called 911. Looking down at his pockets she seen the box falling out. She grabbed it and opened it.

"GOD PLEASE DON'T DO THIS TO ME!!!" She screamed. She grabbed the ring out the box and put it on her hand.

She looked backed down at JaKai. "YES I'M GOING TO MARRY YOU AND YOURE NOT GOING TO LEAVE ME AND YOUR BABIES. I LOVE YOU SO MUCH JAKIA I NEED YOU! WE NEED YOU." She told him.

JaKai smiled, blood poured from his mouth, his chest heaved up and faintly fell down, he took his last breath.

"JAKAI! JAKAI! PLEASEEEEEEE!" Nia cried.

JaKai died in her lap. Nia wrapped her arms around him while her kids sat in the car crying their hearts out as if they knew their daddy was no longer going to be there. What JaKai and Nia had, the love, the incredible bond between the two of them was something that some would kill for.

Nia didn't want to let JaKai go, her heart was crushed in millions of pieces and there was no repairing it. Life was perfect for her until someone decided to ruin everything she had. She felt like her beginning was quickly snatched away and now it was her ending....

Please don't forget to leave your review and check out other books by me! www.staceystaxx.com connect with me on FaceBook @ Stacey Staxx or Alexus Stacey Staxx. The official Pen Slayer. Thank you!

Star City Publications

www.starcitypublications.com

Envy The Root Of All Evil 1

Envy The Root Of All Evil 2

Envy The Root Of All Evil 3

Envy The Root Of All Evil 4

Pretty Money

Gold Diggin Honeys

Momma I Ain't No Saint

Raven's Cravings Book

Raven's Cravings movie

The Bentleys

The Perfect Side Nigga

Hell Between My Thighs

FOU

Love On LockDown

Ryder: Every Thug Needs A Ryder

Untamed & Deranged Mates

The Streets Can Wait But My Love Won't

Almighty Dollar

Hell In My Life…Real Rap

Sins Of A Pastor

Quiet Storm

The Book Of Syn

The Thrill

Low Down & Dirty Lovers 1

Low Down & Dirty Lovers 2